The Bible: Evaluating Patterns

Patmos Publishing

books@patmosmedia.com

The Bible: Evaluating Patterns

Patmos Isle Publishing

www.troyshaw.com

ACKNOWLEDGEMENTS

I am more than appreciative for my proofreaders Cathy Palmer, Epris Curry, Kelly Shaw, and the entire Patmos Isle Publishing family.

DEDICATION

I dedicate this book to the God of Abraham, Isaac, Jacob, my father, and my father's father. With heartfelt admiration, this book is dedicated to my friend and teacher Professor Reuben Ahroni.

PREFACE

I wrote this book in order to present part of what I see when studying the Biblical text. It seems more than fascinating to me that there is a pattern weaved into each passage – we just have to have our eyes analytically and spiritually open to see the paradigm. Furthermore, it seems to me that we can see glimpses of God as the pattern is revealed throughout the scripture.

In my travels and work many opportunities to teach students to see the patterns have emerged, bringing forth the great fruit of enlightenment. Although it has been a pleasure to serve as a pattern tour guide through lectures – it has seemed extremely difficult to present the patterns upon a literary platform. Additionally, the feeling that students should be raising their hands with questions seemed anonymously present as I was writing. Unfortunately, the opportunity to take questions has not been realistically manifested; therefore my hope is that this writing may open opportunities for dialog with readers. Of course I will not be able to come with a personal lecture to converse with every individual reader – therefore it is encouraged that you engage a duotone discourse with the scripture and the Holy Spirit within.

This book is penned in order to encourage you to look for the powerful patterns within the Biblical text, although many of my favorites will be presented within this book – there is an enumerable mass of threads within God's pattern. Although, this work will attempt to articulate part of the pattern into the restriction of the written language – one must realize that the pattern is a super special visual art, which must be viewed through spiritual eyes dependent on divine light. My great hope is for readers to gain an appreciation for God as a glimpse of the greatest love shimmers within the light of the scripture.

Please do not be alarmed at the very small print, a decision had to be made – in order to print all of the scripture the font has been reduced. The scripture is there to help you, please do not allow it to alter your focus. If the print is too small – then please use your Bible as a companion to the book. Each page has a cost, and stewardship is a factor – therefore keeping the overall cost down allows a greater number of readers to afford the book. Thank you for understanding and may the Lord bless you as you continue to grow in the light.

The Bible: Evaluating Patterns

Patmos Isle Publishing

www.troyshaw.com

The Bible: Evaluating Patterns

INTRODUCTION

I have a rare type of an early onset presbyopia optical condition, which causes my eyes to work really hard to bring objects into focus – especially when close up. The strain of focus became painful during my graduate school years from all of the reading, after about 500 pages my eyes would start to burn. I went to several optometrists, yet they could not find any issues with my eyes.

It took a highly trained specialist and extraordinary diagnostic equipment to detect my misaligned focal point. Normally when there are issues with sight the doctor prescribes glasses although my form of presbyopia may be eased with glasses, they will not singularly fix the

3

problem. The doctor prescribed several optical exercises to strengthen my eyes. Most of the exercises consisted of searching for patterns and adjusting distances with my eyes – look close then far away kind of thing.

It is more than interesting to me how God uses patterns in our lives – we are set up for the future long before arriving there, as the resources that we need have already been provided for us even before we understand them. Just as Moses was drawn out of the water as a baby – I have had the opportunity to triumph through presbyopia by looking for hidden patterns. It seems that the Lord was preparing me in graduate school to seek patterns on many levels – further still I can remember as a child taking toys apart to see how they work.

This book is a collection of writings that present a few of my observations with regards to God's patterns. There are five major themes that you should look for throughout your reading:

- Seed
- Tabernacle/Temple
- Light
- Water
- Wind

These five themes are important and I do not want to diminish their symbolism, yet I would prefer that you keep your mind open to the pattern over the symbols. In the simplest terms just think about the equation 2+2=4, if we focus on the numbers we will never know anything more than the sum of 2 and 2, on the other hand if we focus on the equation we are empowered to change the variables in order to see greater sums. I sincerely hope that you find my references to be interesting and thought provoking, however the presence of the pattern is the overarching theme.

During the daily optical exercises there were times of frustration, as the hidden picture would not immediately emerge for my eyes to see – therefore diligence was required. This book will necessitate your faithfulness, especially if you are new to the paradigm – hopefully by the third chapter things will start to come together. Please do not give up on the patterns, keep reading with your spiritual eyes wide open – but do not be afraid to look away if you need to rest your eyes for a moment and them come back to focus again.

Additionally, be warned that even though this book is about divine patterns – very little will be said with regards to finding them. The writings will not necessarily give you a step by step how to guide, as a matter of fact you may become confused but if you remain faithful to read on, by the end you will be a part of the pattern. I have purposely left the book open for you to work and think. Several transitional paragraphs have been omitted, as your skills will be sharpened through the effort required to embrace the paradigm. It is up to you to put all of the information together in order to see the magnified picture of God. For some it may be instant and for others it may take some serious re-focusing, but I can assure you that the pattern can be found.

They say that sex sales, and if that is the case then the first chapter should be interesting. We will start our exploration of the pattern with Adam, Eve, and the seed. Pay close attention to the planting of the seed, because the book journeys from the concrete to the abstract if viewed from mere carnal minds seeking mental cognition. Seed requires a place to be planted, light, water, and harvest. If you detect the pattern then the application will follow. Although the writing articulates part of the seedtime and harvest process, the main attraction should be God. I would contend that no matter the scripture, we should be able to see that pattern of God.

Hopefully you will be encouraged to keep seeking the love, peace, grace, mercy, and joy of God through embracing the collective of the scriptures. The way of God can be seen throughout the scriptures, however the best view is found upon the summit of reading the entire Bible from Genesis to Revelation. The collective pattern will reveal God in ways that you cannot imagine. Hopefully the words within this work will testify to the particular care that God has put forth toward us and spark a desire to embrace the pattern to the extent that your life will become altered at the altar within you.

IT IS MORE THAN SEX:

ADAM & EVE

Genesis 1:1-3:24 *In the beginning God created the heaven and the earth. 2 And the earth was without form, and void; and darkness was upon the face of the deep. And the Spirit of God moved upon the face of the waters. 3 And God said, Let there be light: and there was light. 4 And God saw the light, that it was good: and God divided the light from the darkness. 5 And God called the light Day, and the darkness he called Night. And the evening and the morning were the first day. 6 And God said, Let there be a firmament in the midst of the waters, and let it divide the waters from the waters. 7 And God made the firmament, and divided the waters which were under the firmament from the waters which were above the firmament: and it was so. 8 And God called the firmament Heaven. And the evening and the morning were the second day. 9 And God said, Let the waters under the heaven be gathered together unto one place, and let the dry land appear: and it was so. 10 And God called the dry land Earth; and the gathering together of the waters called he Seas: and God saw that it was good. 11 And God said, Let the earth bring forth grass, the herb yielding seed, and the fruit tree yielding fruit after his kind, whose seed is in itself, upon the earth: and it was so. 12 And the earth brought forth grass, and herb yielding seed after his kind, and the tree yielding fruit, whose seed was in itself, after his kind: and God saw that it was good. 13 And the evening and the morning were the third day. 14 And God said, Let there be lights in the firmament of the heaven to divide the day from the night; and let them be for signs, and for seasons, and for days, and years: 15 And*

2

let them be for lights in the firmament of the heaven to give light upon the earth: and it was so. 16 And God made two great lights; the greater light to rule the day, and the lesser light to rule the night: he made the stars also. 17 And God set them in the firmament of the heaven to give light upon the earth, 18 And to rule over the day and over the night, and to divide the light from the darkness: and God saw that it was good. 19 And the evening and the morning were the fourth day. 20 And God said, Let the waters bring forth abundantly the moving creature that hath life, and fowl that may fly above the earth in the open firmament of heaven. 21 And God created great whales, and every living creature that moveth, which the waters brought forth abundantly, after their kind, and every winged fowl after his kind: and God saw that it was good. 22 And God blessed them, saying, Be fruitful, and multiply, and fill the waters in the seas, and let fowl multiply in the earth. 23 And the evening and the morning were the fifth day. 24 And God said, Let the earth bring forth the living creature after his kind, cattle, and creeping thing, and beast of the earth after his kind: and it was so. 25 And God made the beast of the earth after his kind, and cattle after their kind, and every thing that creepeth upon the earth after his kind: and God saw that it was good. 26 And God said, Let us make man in our image, after our likeness: and let them have dominion over the fish of the sea, and over the fowl of the air, and over the cattle, and over all the earth, and over every creeping thing that creepeth upon the earth. 27 So God created man in his own image, in the image of God created he him; male and female created he them. 28 And God blessed them, and God said unto them, Be fruitful, and multiply, and replenish the earth, and subdue it: and have dominion over the fish of the sea, and over the fowl of the air, and over every living thing that moveth upon the earth. 29 And God said, Behold, I have given you every herb bearing seed, which is upon the face of all the earth, and every tree, in the which is the fruit of a tree yielding seed; to you it shall be for meat. 30 And to every beast of the earth, and to every fowl of the air, and to every thing that creepeth upon the earth, wherein there is life, I have given every green herb for meat: and it was so. 31 And God saw every thing that he had made, and, behold, it was very good. And the evening and the morning were the sixth day. 2:1 Thus the heavens and the earth were finished, and all the host of them. 2 And on the seventh day God ended his work which he had made; and he rested on the seventh day from all his work which he had made. 3 And God blessed the seventh day, and sanctified it: because that in it he had rested from all his work which God created and made. 4 These are the generations of the heavens and of the earth when they were created, in the day that the LORD God made the earth and the heavens, 5 And every plant of the field before it was in the earth, and every herb of the field before it grew: for the LORD God had not caused it to rain upon the earth, and there was not a man to till the ground. 6 But there went up a mist from the earth, and watered the whole face of the ground. 7 And the LORD God formed man of the dust of the ground, and breathed into his nostrils the breath of life; and man became a living soul. 8 And the LORD God planted a garden eastward in Eden; and there he put the man whom he had formed. 9 And out of the ground made the LORD God to grow every tree that is pleasant to the sight, and good for food; the tree of life also in the midst of the garden, and the tree of knowledge of good and evil. 10 And a river went out of Eden to water the garden; and from thence it was parted, and became into four heads. 11 The name of the first is Pison: that is it which compasseth the whole land of Havilah, where there is gold; 12 And the gold of that land is good: there is bdellium and the onyx stone. 13 And the name of the second river is Gihon: the same is it that compasseth the whole land of Ethiopia. 14 And the name of the third river is Hiddekel: that is it which goeth toward the east of Assyria. And the fourth river is Euphrates. 15 And the LORD God took the man, and put him into the garden of Eden to dress it and to keep it. 16 And the LORD God commanded the man, saying, Of every tree of the garden thou mayest freely eat: 17 But of the tree of the knowledge of good and evil, thou shalt not eat of it: for in the day that thou eatest thereof thou shalt surely die. 18 And the LORD God said, It is not good that the man should be alone; I will make him an help meet for him. 19 And out of the ground the LORD God formed every beast of the field, and every fowl of the air; and brought them unto Adam to see what he would call them: and whatsoever Adam called every living creature, that was the name thereof. 20 And Adam gave names to all cattle, and to the fowl of the air, and to every beast of the field; but for Adam there was not found an help meet for him. 21 And the LORD God caused a deep sleep to fall upon Adam, and he slept: and he took one of his ribs, and closed up the flesh instead thereof; 22 And the rib, which the LORD God had taken from man, made he a woman, and brought her unto the man. 23 And Adam said, This is now bone of my bones, and flesh of my flesh: she shall be called Woman, because she was taken out of Man. 24 Therefore shall a man leave his father and his mother, and shall cleave unto his wife: and they shall be one flesh. 25 And they were both naked, the man and his wife, and were not ashamed. 3:1 Now the serpent was more subtil than any beast of the field which the LORD God had made. And he said unto the woman, Yea, hath God said, Ye shall not eat of every tree of the garden? 2 And the woman said unto the serpent, We may eat of the fruit of the trees of the garden: 3 But of the fruit of the tree which is in the midst of the garden, God hath said, Ye shall not eat of it, neither shall ye touch it, lest ye die. 4 And the serpent said unto the woman, Ye shall not surely die: 5 For God doth know that in the day ye eat thereof, then your eyes shall be opened, and ye shall be as gods, knowing good and evil. 6 And when the woman saw that the tree was good for food, and that it was pleasant to the eyes, and a tree to be desired to make one wise, she took of the fruit thereof, and did eat, and gave also unto her husband with her; and he did eat. 7 And the eyes of them both were opened, and they knew that they were naked; and they sewed fig leaves together, and made themselves aprons. 8 And they heard the voice of the LORD God walking in the garden in the cool of the day:

6

and Adam and his wife hid themselves from the presence of the LORD God amongst the trees of the garden. 9 And the LORD God called unto Adam, and said unto him, Where art thou? 10 And he said, I heard thy voice in the garden, and I was afraid, because I was naked; and I hid myself. 11 And he said, Who told thee that thou wast naked? Hast thou eaten of the tree, whereof I commanded thee that thou shouldest not eat? 12 And the man said, The woman whom thou gavest to be with me, she gave me of the tree, and I did eat. 13 And the LORD God said unto the woman, What is this that thou hast done? And the woman said, The serpent beguiled me, and I did eat. 14 And the LORD God said unto the serpent, Because thou hast done this, thou art cursed above all cattle, and above every beast of the field; upon thy belly shalt thou go, and dust shalt thou eat all the days of thy life: 15 And I will put enmity between thee and the woman, and between thy seed and her seed; it shall bruise thy head, and thou shalt bruise his heel. 16 Unto the woman he said, I will greatly multiply thy sorrow and thy conception; in sorrow thou shalt bring forth children; and thy desire shall be to thy husband, and he shall rule over thee. 17 And unto Adam he said, Because thou hast hearkened unto the voice of thy wife, and hast eaten of the tree, of which I commanded thee, saying, Thou shalt not eat of it: cursed is the ground for thy sake; in sorrow shalt thou eat of it all the days of thy life; 18 Thorns also and thistles shall it bring forth to thee; and thou shalt eat the herb of the field; 19 In the sweat of thy face shalt thou eat bread, till thou return unto the ground; for out of it wast thou *taken: for dust thou art, and unto dust shalt thou return. 20 And Adam called his wife's name Eve; because she was the mother of all living. 21 Unto Adam also and to his wife did the LORD God make coats of skins, and clothed them. 22 And the LORD God said, Behold, the man is become as one of us, to know good and evil: and now, lest he put forth his hand, and take also of the tree of life, and eat, and live for ever: 23 Therefore the LORD God sent him forth from the garden of Eden, to till the ground from whence he was taken. 24 So he drove out the man; and he placed at the east of the garden of Eden Cherubims, and a flaming sword which turned every way, to keep the way of the tree of life.*

Most of us are familiar with the fall of man, Adam and Eve sinned as they disobeyed God, and were subsequently put out of the Garden of Eden. Their sin caused them to discover their nakedness, therefore God clothes them in Genesis 3:21[1] (coats of skins). They recognized in Genesis

---

[1] *Genesis 3:21   Unto Adam also and to his wife did the LORD God make coats of skins, and clothed them.*

8

3:7[2] that they were in a different state – they were afraid because they were naked, therefore God gave them animal skins to cover themselves. An animal had to die in order to cover the fallen couple.

The death of the animal sets a precedence for sacrifice and salvation – which created a pattern. Even though they had disobeyed, God still sees fit to cover them; nevertheless they had to endure consequences. Parents may learn a lesson from God, in that even when our children are disobedient there should be balance with consequences – we should never leave them completely naked to their mistakes even in their disobedience.

---

[2] *Genesis 3:7 And the eyes of them both were opened, and they knew that they were naked; and they sewed fig leaves together, and made themselves aprons.*

The garden experience created many suboptimal results for humankind. In chapters 1 and 2 of Genesis we can see one of the issues here is that now when we come together intimately in marriage, we are becoming nearly like God more so than any other time with regards to our ability to create. Before the transgression of the fallen family, God was personally crafting humans with His own hands, making full provisions for life, without the pain and struggles of creation being felt by man and woman. After Adam and Eve transgressed they were upon the portals of discovery. God is a creator, and does not like to destroy (remembering the animal that had to die in order to create coverings for Adam and Eve). God creates, and we have been given the ability to create, in the image of God we have been given the functional ability to create.

More specific, it seems notable that the first offspring of humankind was crafted from man through surgical means, post-garden the pains of birth now remain with woman. I wonder if un-natural child birth is a further indication toward a declining relationship and disrespect toward God by humankind. Perhaps some of our children's illnesses and behavioral challenges stem from attempting to escape child birth as naturally intended. Early on we can see the problems of fornication and sexual immorality, as there seems to be a struggle with blended families throughout the scriptures (this will become concretized as we examine familial patterns). The pattern of sexuality (creation) is divinely sacred – let me explain; if you remember in the beginning God created the heavens and the earth – He moved across the darkness and the face of the deep.

Think about the female anatomy, and the fact that her sexual organ is steeped in darkness, and there is an abyss (dark hole) if you will. When a husband and wife come together, the husband comes across the face of the deep and then some light is shed as the opening is embarked upon. Then just as in creation the waters come together, later separating waters from mass become dividing atoms. Just as God separated the land from the waters, so in the womb similar events occur as out of the dark abyss a pattern of life emerges. When God came to create, He first shed light upon the abyss of darkness, and so when husband and wife come together it is very similar to creation from the foundation of Biblical creation. God sheds light on the face of the deep, upon the waters, and creates something out of nothingness. When the husband comes together with the wife, light is shed upon darkness and waters (fluid) comes together to create something from virtually nothing.

Although science attempts to explain this process through the vigor of mitosis and the embryonic process – at the end of the day this is purely miraculous and divine. There is nothing, as each of us has been formed from nothing, but darkness and fluid – nothingness transforms into body and soul. It is more than important that we recognize that our body should be the temple of the Holy Spirit a living place of sacrifice. It seems to me that this is why fornication is the only time whereby our bodies are involved in sin which we will explore later. The function of creation with our bodies is a great gift that the Lord gave us; we should recognize the sacred responsibility to protect the process.

In Genesis chapter 3, God makes them clothes and issues consequences to their disobedience. Their punishment in a sense was to discover the challenges of God as creator and provider. God gives them the ability to create through the husband wife relationship (Adam must provide and Eve must conceive) – they want to be gods – so God gives them a little taste of what that means; seemingly so that they may empathize with Him. Their desire to be like God seems to remain at the root of our sinful nature – when we decide that we want to be in control the final outcome is consistently detrimental. God has given us the ability to have and raise children, just as He created and is raising us. As we reflect that Adam and Eve sinned, God clothes them, as an animal dies to provide them with coverings – and so we can see there is a cost to sin; and now we have an early formula and foreshadow of sacrifice.

SEEING A RAM KNOWING THE FUTURE: ABRAHAM & ISAAC

Genesis 22:1-24 And it came to pass after these things, that God did tempt Abraham, and said unto him, Abraham: and he said, Behold, here I am. 2 And he said, Take now thy son, thine only son Isaac, whom thou lovest, and get thee into the land of Moriah; and offer him there for a burnt offering upon one of the mountains which I will tell thee of. 3 And Abraham rose up early in the morning, and saddled his ass, and took two of his young men with him, and Isaac his son, and clave the wood for the burnt offering, and rose up, and went unto the place of which God had told him. 4 Then on the third day Abraham lifted up his eyes, and saw the place afar off. 5 And Abraham said unto his young men, Abide ye here with the ass; and I and the lad will go yonder and worship, and come again to you. 6 And Abraham took the wood of the burnt offering, and laid it upon Isaac his son; and he took the fire in his hand, and a knife; and they went both of them together. 7 And Isaac spake unto Abraham his father, and said, My father: and he said, Here am I, my son. And he said, Behold the fire and the wood: but where is the lamb for a burnt offering? 8 And Abraham said, My son, God will provide himself a lamb for a burnt offering: so they went both of them together. 9 And they came to the place which God had told him of; and Abraham built an altar there, and laid the wood in order, and bound Isaac his son, and laid him on the altar upon the wood. 10 And Abraham stretched forth his hand, and took the knife to slay his son. 11 And the angel of the LORD called unto him out of heaven, and said, Abraham, Abraham: and he said, Here am I. 12 And he said, Lay not thine hand upon the lad, neither do thou any thing unto him: for now I know that thou fearest God, seeing thou hast not withheld thy son, thine only son from me. 13 And Abraham lifted up his eyes, and looked, and behold behind him a ram caught in a thicket by his horns: and Abraham went and took the ram, and offered him up for a burnt offering in the stead of his son. 14 And Abraham called the name of that place Jehovahjireh: as it is said to this day, In the mount of the LORD it shall be seen. 15 And the angel of the LORD called unto Abraham out of heaven the second time, 16 And said, By myself have I sworn, saith the LORD, for because thou hast done this thing, and hast not withheld thy son, thine only son: 17 That in blessing I will bless thee, and in multiplying I will multiply thy seed as the stars of the heaven, and as the sand which is upon the sea shore; and thy seed shall possess the gate of his enemies; 18 And in thy seed shall all the nations of the earth be blessed; because thou hast obeyed my voice. 19 So Abraham returned unto his young men, and they rose up and went together to Beersheba; and Abraham dwelt at Beersheba. 20 And it came to pass after these things, that it was told Abraham, saying, Behold, Milcah, she hath also born children unto thy brother Nahor; 21 Huz his firstborn, and Buz his brother, and Kemuel the father of Aram, 22 And Chesed, and Hazo, and Pildash, and Jidlaph, and Bethuel. 23 And Bethuel begat Rebekah: these eight Milcah did bear to Nahor, Abraham's brother. 24 And his concubine, whose name was Reumah, she bare also Tebah, and Gaham, and Thahash, and Maachah.

In Genesis 22:4 we can see more of the pre-configuration of salvation as related to sacrifice. Here we see Abraham with his only son from marriage, on the third day, in a mountain, with two servants, and wood. Similarly, on a hill called Calvary there was an only born son, approaching a three day episode, with wood, and two men.

In Genesis 24:7[3] Isaac is questioning his father as to the whereabouts of the sacrifice, like many of us when we are blind to the fact that we are facing death – Isaac is oblivious toward encroaching destruction. Interestingly enough, Isaac was being led by his father, similarly to the way that Abraham was being led by his

---

[3] *Genesis 3:7 And the eyes of them both were opened, and they knew that they were naked; and they sewed fig leaves together, and made themselves aprons.*

Heavenly Father. We may not always be aware of what God is up to, but we can always rest assured that everything will be alright – if we leave the details up to Him.

In Genesis 22:10[4] Abraham is about to sacrifice his son, when in Genesis 22:11[5], an angel stopped him and in Genesis 24:13[6] there was a ram caught in the thickets – as we can see early on in the scripture, our Christ crowned with thorns to take our place as sacrifice to cover our debt. The pattern of the text shows us that the pattern of salvation did not start just a few years

---

[4] *Genesis 22:10 And Abraham stretched forth his hand, and took the knife to slay his son.*

[5] *Genesis 22:11 And the angel of the LORD called unto him out of heaven, and said, Abraham, Abraham: and he said, Here am I.*

[6] *Genesis 22:13 And Abraham lifted up his eyes, and looked, and behold behind him a ram caught in a thicket by his horns: and Abraham went and took the ram, and offered him up for a burnt offering in the stead of his son.*

ago, but God's love is so great that our deliverance began in the garden and the pattern continues to contribute to the greatest narrative of love. God was thinking about us even before we messed up ("anointing" if you will, ever present preparation), as we can see remnants of sacrifice provided for our salvation. Are we willing to embrace God, as He has been working to save us from the very beginning of our struggles with satanic forces?

We can see throughout the scriptures little events that lead to our salvation. The obstacles that you may be going through right now, the little events that happen in your life from day to day – are merely opportunities for you to watch the work of God in your journey. Even when we don't see the fullness of God's plan – we must trust and believe that the Lord is here; just as He was there for Abraham in that thicket waiting to provide a sacrificial gift to save our future.

THE TENT CHURCH

Exodus 25:1-40 And the LORD spake unto Moses, saying, 2 Speak unto the children of Israel, that they bring me an offering: of every man that giveth it willingly with his heart ye shall take my offering. 3 And this is the offering which ye shall take of them; gold, and silver, and brass, 4 And blue, and purple, and scarlet, and fine linen, and goats' hair, 5 And rams' skins dyed red, and badgers' skins, and shittim wood, 6 Oil for the light, spices for anointing oil, and for sweet incense, 7 Onyx stones, and stones to be set in the ephod, and in the breastplate. 8 And let them make me a sanctuary; that I may dwell among them. 9 According to all that I shew thee, after the pattern of the tabernacle, and the pattern of all the instruments thereof, even so shall ye make it. 10 And they shall make an ark of shittim wood: two cubits and a half shall be the length thereof, and a cubit and a half the breadth thereof, and a cubit and a half the height thereof. 11 And thou shalt overlay it with pure gold, within and without shalt thou overlay it, and shalt make upon it a crown of gold round about. 12 And thou shalt cast four rings of gold for it, and put them in the four corners thereof; and two rings shall be in the one side of it, and two rings in the other side of it. 13 And thou shalt make staves of shittim wood, and overlay them with gold. 14 And thou shalt put the staves into the rings by the sides of the ark, that the ark may be borne with them. 15 The staves shall be in the rings of the ark: they shall not be taken from it. 16 And thou shalt put into the ark the testimony which I shall give thee. 17 And thou shalt make a mercy seat of pure gold: two cubits and a half shall be the length thereof, and a cubit and a half the breadth thereof. 18 And thou shalt make two cherubims of gold, of beaten work shalt thou make them, in the two

24

ends of the mercy seat. 19 And make one cherub on the one end, and the other cherub on the other end: even of the mercy seat shall ye make the cherubims on the two ends thereof. 20 And the cherubims shall stretch forth their wings on high, covering the mercy seat with their wings, and their faces shall look one to another; toward the mercy seat shall the faces of the cherubims be. 21 And thou shalt put the mercy seat above upon the ark; and in the ark thou shalt put the testimony that I shall give thee. 22 And there I will meet with thee, and I will commune with thee from above the mercy seat, from between the two cherubims which are upon the ark of the testimony, of all things which I will give thee in commandment unto the children of Israel. 23 Thou shalt also make a table of shittim wood: two cubits shall be the length thereof, and a cubit the breadth thereof, and a cubit and a half the height thereof. 24 And thou shalt overlay it with pure gold, and make thereto a crown of gold round about. 25 And thou shalt make unto it a border of an hand breadth round about, and thou shalt make a golden crown to the border thereof round about. 26 And thou shalt make for it four rings of gold, and put the rings in the four corners that are on the four feet thereof. 27 Over against the border shall the rings be for places of the staves to bear the table. 28 And thou shalt make the staves of shittim wood, and overlay them with gold, that the table may be borne with them. 29 And thou shalt make the dishes thereof, and spoons thereof, and covers thereof, and bowls thereof, to cover withal: of pure gold shalt thou make them. 30 And thou shalt set upon the table shewbread before me alway. 31 And thou shalt make a candlestick of pure gold: of beaten work shall the candlestick be made: his shaft, and his branches, his *bowls, his knops, and his flowers, shall be of the same. 32 And six branches shall come out of the sides of it; three branches of the candlestick out of the one side, and three branches of the candlestick out of the other side: 33 Three bowls made like unto almonds, with a knop and a flower in one branch; and three bowls made like almonds in the other branch, with a knop and a flower: so in the six branches that come out of the candlestick. 34 And in the candlestick shall be four bowls made like unto almonds, with their knops and their flowers. 35 And there shall be a knop under two branches of the same, and a knop under two branches of the same, and a knop under two branches of the same, according to the six branches that proceed out of the candlestick. 36 Their knops and their branches shall be of the same: all it shall be one beaten work of pure gold. 37 And thou shalt make the seven lamps thereof: and they shall light the lamps thereof, that they may give light over against it. 38 And the tongs thereof, and the snuffdishes thereof, shall be of pure gold. 39 Of a talent of pure gold shall he make it, with all these vessels. 40 And look that thou make them after their pattern, which was shewed thee in the mount.*

We must prepare a place of sacrifice and worship for God. In Exodus 25:8, God tells them to make a sanctuary so that He might dwell among them. He wanted them to prepare a place of worship using His pattern – here we can see that there is a pattern to God; a plan if you will. God does not just haphazardly work, but there is a pattern. The beauty of the pattern seems to be that we can often embrace fortified faith in God's way. We have the ability to recognize God prophetically, but part of the way that we may recognize him prophetically is to fully understand Him historically – if you want to know what will happen next, most often all you have to do is start asking what happened last. Because God works in patterns, we can see Him in the future by, studying Him in the past. Because God works in patterns, we have the ability to avoid the trap of shallow spiritualism.

Part of the way that we know the voice of the Holy Spirit, is that first and foremost Christ said that the Spirit would never speak of Himself. The Holy Spirit only speaks of what has already been spoken, therefore if our spirit is contrary to God's word then we should automatically know that we are not being led by the Holy Spirit. At times it is difficult to discern the voice of God from other voices, however if we continue to check the pattern found in scripture, we will then know the voice of the Lord.

We should worship in a place of pattern, a tabernacle that is built from the pattern of God. Let me take you back - when Adam and Eve stepped out of God's pattern in the garden, they began to feel uncomfortable, and their nakedness bothered them. When we step outside of God's pattern we should be bothered, notice that we live in a world whereby the profane has become celebrated and profanity has become the order of modern society. What my grandmother referred to as strange sex, has now become a part of socio-normative conversation.

Adam and Eve were ashamed of their nakedness, because they had stepped outside of the order of God – think about our modern society and the celebration of nakedness. People seem to be more than proud of their fleshly bodies – nakedness is all around. Women and men seem to wear more and more revealing clothing, and to make matters worse, many people don't even care how they are shaped (spandex should be outlawed, and for some it should carry a mandatory prison sentence). People don't care about their sin, proud of nakedness and profanity – stepping outside of

the pattern of God. Furthermore, there is this
keep it all the way real attitude – whereby people
are mentally naked, meaning that we should not
feel comfortable with revealing everything that is
on our minds. There was an age whereby people
guarded their conversation. Now it seems that
people say whatever they feel, whenever they
feel like opening their mouth. There seems to be
no perimeters on conversation, even with regards
to young people – topics that used to be off limits
for children to say and/or hear are now a part of
the daily vernacular.

Additionally, we seem to live within a culture
where our social lives are naked – with the
inception of social media, people freely place
their lives before the world; there are no curtains
adorning the windows of our lives. Our dietary

discourse, along with our location and logistic log seem public place, along with sexuality – coupled with continual emotional status. We are naked, with the exception of a bit of ink here and there – which seems to provide motivation for renewed nakedness.

The text seems to suggest that prideful nakedness is profane and perverse. Foundationally, God has done so much to keep us covered; it seems disrespectful to embrace nudity as a way of life. Nudity often fosters lustful thoughts that germinate into lustful actions. It is difficult to remain focused in the modern society, as sexual images and tones are environmentally hazardous toward the sober minded. Jacob made a coat of many colors as a gift for his son Joseph[7] – his brothers took it before they sold him. Potiphar's wife later took another coat from Joseph[8], before she had him sent to prison, Noah's nakedness was caused by intoxication[9], David was found naked and upset Saul's daughter[10], Bathsheba[11] was naked and sparked David's murderous actions. People tore their clothes within the Bible to denote sadness and mourning, and the Romans took the robe of Christ during the time of crucifixion – it seems that negative events are often parallel with the loss of clothing within the Bible.

In Exodus 25, God gives us the first part of the solution – He has the Hebrews to come together to build the tabernacle together. God has them to

---

[7] Genesis Chapter 37
[8] Genesis Chapter 39
[9] Genesis 9:21
[10] 2 Samuel 6:15-16
[11] 2 Samuel 11:1-4

collect materials from everybody, so that all could actively participate in the construction. We must come together and embrace the way of God, as we create a place of sanctuary collectively. It costs the community something in order to create a place of tabernacle. We must be willing to give up something in order to come into relationship with God. In order for us to get back to the place where God wants us to be, in a right relationship with Him and each other, it must start with each of us actively embracing a pattern that promotes the community of worship. We must begin to cover each other, through prayer and spiritual motivation, sharing the scriptures as the Holy Spirit leads us.

The tabernacle was to be built using the best materials that were fortified to last. Our community of faith should seek to place our very best into worship, missions, and ministry. Our connection with God and each other must be built to endure the trials of time; therefore the word of God (His pattern) must remain at the forefront of all that we do. Far too often our community of faith has been enticed by the naked world, and we have begun to be infected rather than becoming effective. We must carry out God's plan from the solid rock, just as the wood and gold provided for the tabernacle were elements of excellence – we should be committed to the same pattern of greatness.

FROM WHEAT TO WITNESSES:

SIN TO SALVATION

1 Chronicles 21:1-30   And Satan stood up against Israel, and provoked David to number Israel. 2   And David said to Joab and to the rulers of the people, Go, number Israel from Beersheba even to Dan; and bring the number of them to me, that I may know it. 3 And Joab answered, The LORD make his people an hundred times so many more as they be: but, my lord the king, are they not all my lord's servants? why then doth my lord require this thing? why will he be a cause of trespass to Israel? 4 Nevertheless the king's word prevailed against Joab. Wherefore Joab departed, and went throughout all Israel, and came to Jerusalem. 5 And Joab gave the sum of the number of the people unto David. And all they of Israel were a thousand thousand and an hundred thousand men that drew sword: and Judah was four hundred threescore and ten thousand men that drew sword. 6 But Levi and Benjamin counted he not among them: for the king's word was abominable to Joab. 7 And God was displeased with this thing; therefore he smote Israel. 8 And David said unto God, I have sinned greatly, because I have done this thing: but now, I beseech thee, do away the iniquity of thy servant; for I have done very foolishly. 9 And the LORD spake unto Gad, David's seer, saying, 10   Go and tell David, saying, Thus saith the LORD, I offer thee three things: choose thee one of them, that I may do it unto thee. 11 So Gad came to David, and said unto him, Thus saith the LORD, Choose thee   12   Either three years' famine; or three months to be destroyed before thy foes, while that the sword of thine enemies overtaketh thee; or else three days the sword of the LORD, even the pestilence, in the land, and the angel of the LORD destroying throughout all the coasts of Israel. Now therefore advise thyself what word I shall bring again to him that sent me. 13 And David said unto Gad, I am in a great strait: let me fall now into the hand of the LORD; for very great are his mercies: but let me not fall into the hand of man. 14 So the LORD sent pestilence upon Israel: and there fell of Israel seventy thousand men. 15 And God sent an angel unto Jerusalem to destroy it: and as he was destroying, the LORD beheld, and he repented him of the evil, and said to the angel that destroyed, It is enough, stay now thine hand. And the angel of the LORD stood by the threshingfloor of Ornan the Jebusite. 16 And David lifted up his eyes, and saw the angel of the LORD stand between the earth and the heaven, having a drawn sword in his hand stretched out over Jerusalem. Then David and the elders of Israel, who were clothed in sackcloth, fell upon their faces. 17 And David said unto God, Is it not I that commanded the people to be numbered? even I it is that have sinned and done evil indeed; but as for these sheep, what have they done? let thine hand, I pray thee, O LORD my God, be on me, and on my father's house; but not on thy people, that they should be plagued. 18 Then the angel of the LORD commanded Gad to say to David, that David should go up, and set up an altar unto the LORD in the threshingfloor of Ornan the Jebusite. 19 And David went up at the saying of Gad, which he spake in the name of the LORD. 20 And Ornan turned back, and saw the angel; and his four sons with him hid themselves. Now Ornan was threshing wheat. 21 And as David came to Ornan, Ornan looked and saw David, and went out of the threshingfloor, and bowed himself to David with his face to the ground. 22 Then David said to Ornan, Grant me the place of this threshingfloor, that I may build an altar therein unto the

37

LORD: thou shalt grant it me for the full price: that the plague
may be stayed from the people. 23 And Ornan said unto David,
Take it to thee, and let my lord the king do that which is good in
his eyes: lo, I give thee the oxen also for burnt offerings, and the
threshing instruments for wood, and the wheat for the meat
offering; I give it all. 24 And king David said to Ornan, Nay; but
I will verily buy it for the full price: for I will not take that which is
thine for the LORD, nor offer burnt offerings without cost. 25 So
David gave to Ornan for the place six hundred shekels of gold by
weight. 26 And David built there an altar unto the LORD, and
offered burnt offerings and peace offerings, and called upon the
LORD; and he answered him from heaven by fire upon the altar of
burnt offering. 27 And the LORD commanded the angel; and he
put up his sword again into the sheath thereof. 28 At that time
when David saw that the LORD had answered him in the
threshingfloor of Ornan the Jebusite, then he sacrificed there. 29
For the tabernacle of the LORD, which Moses made in the
wilderness, and the altar of the burnt offering, were at that season
in the high place at Gibeon. 30 But David could not go before it to
enquire of God: for he was afraid because of the sword of the angel
of the LORD.

We must be watchful, because when we seek
to get back to where God wants us to be – satan
often attempts to get back to where he used to be;
because the serpent (satanic symbol) used to

walk upright (Genesis 3:14[12]) – he will stand to appear the same as before; but thank God he can't stand long. In 1 Chronicles 21:1 satan stands up against Israel and provokes David to sin. Even in God's protection, there are times when the enemy will stand up against you – all we have to do is remain in relationship with the Lord; but far too often we choose to stray from the safety zone allowing fear to swallow faith.

We must remain careful not to allow satan to tempt us to act outside of the season and place where God wants us. Although there were times when God allowed the people to be counted (Exodus 30:12[13]), in Chronicles chapter 21 David

---

[12] *Genesis 3:14 And the LORD God said unto the serpent, Because thou hast done this, thou art cursed above all cattle, and above every beast of the field; upon thy belly shalt thou go, and dust shalt thou eat all the days of thy life:*

[13] *Exodus 30:12 When thou takest the sum of the children of Israel after their number, then shall they give every man a ransom for his soul unto the LORD, when*

acts outside of the Lord's desire. There are times when we feel like we have the authority to do something because someone else did it or we were allowed to do it at an earlier time – but no matter what the action, we must act in the timing of God as we are led by the Holy Spirit. There is a time and a season for every action, and it is more than best to humble your steps to the direction of the Holy Spirit. The purpose that God has for your life provides for you to be a uniquely equipped servant of God. Although David does the same thing Moses had been permitted to do earlier, David operates outside of God's desire and gets in trouble.

---

thou numberest them; that there be no plague among them, when thou numberest them.

In 1 Chronicles 21:12[14] David is given three options to provide restitution for his dishonorable action; 1. three years of famine, 2. three months of war, or 3. three days of God's wrath. David embraces the third consequence, wisely understanding that it is far better to be punished by God than man or nature. Although David repents, he still has to endure the consequences of God – and all of the people within David's realm. Remember, as Moses recited the words of God for the people to come together to build the tabernacle – we can see that it is within the pattern of God that we worship in community and now with David's punishment, we can see that there are times when we must

---

[14] *1 Chronicles 21:12   Either three years' famine; or three months to be destroyed before thy foes, while that the sword of thine enemies overtaketh thee; or else three days the sword of the LORD, even the pestilence, in the land, and the angel of the LORD destroying throughout all the coasts of Israel. Now therefore advise thyself what word I shall bring again to him that sent me.*

endure consequences in community. That is why we should not merely think that the sufferings of others are completely disconnected from our life path. We should also recognize the importance of treating our brothers and sisters with respect embracing the importance of community – the pattern of God is that we stand together.

David is found sad and in sackcloth, as he is deeply affected by the suffering of the community – in Chronicles 21:18[15] the remedy emerges from the angel of the Lord, as proclamation is made to Gad, not David. Far too often we foolishly require that God must speak directly to us – and we miss blessings refusing to hear the message of God from divine mediators.

---

[15] *1 Chronicles 21:18 Then the angel of the LORD commanded Gad to say to David, that David should go up, and set up an altar unto the LORD in the threshingfloor of Ornan the Jebusite.*

There are times when the Lord may speak directly to us, but many times He speaks through a messenger. It seems to me that there are times when our sin and defiantly disobedient attitude has separated us from the voice of God – therefore we should be appreciative that the Lord loves us enough to speak; and we should reject the notion that we are worthy to dictate the parameters of God's voice.

David was instructed to purchase a threshing floor, which is a place where grain is roughly refined. A threshing floor is usually a circular, paved, and flat surface, where agriculturalist would thresh/beat the grain harvest and then winnow/expose it to wind. Threshing floors were usually in a high place, to take advantage of calm and consistent winds to facilitate the work of separating the grain from the chaff. After this threshing process, the broken stalks and grain were collected and then thrown up into the air with a wooden fork-like tool called a winnowing fan or they would use flat baskets and toss the stalks into the air. The chaff would be blown away by the wind; the short torn straw would fall some distance away; while the heavier grain would fall at the harvest worker's feet. The grain could then be further separated by sieving/straining. In simple and short, a threshing floor was a place of separation.

Luke 22:31[16] illustrates for us the desire of satan to improperly use God's process. The enemy of all that is good and perfect would like

---

[16] Luke 22:31 *And the Lord said, Simon, Simon, behold, Satan hath desired to have you, that he may sift you as wheat:*

to sift us as wheat, which presents the process, but not the purpose – satan wants to destroy us in the process; God wants to destine us through the process. We must be careful to examine the process that we are going through by the scripture, in order to make sure that we are in the correct pattern. Oftentimes the trick of satan is to present us with a counterfeit that seems right, therefore we must be ever so careful to remain in relationship with God; threshed for triumph rather than sifted for satanic seizure.

Matthew 13:24-30 Another parable put he forth unto them, saying, The kingdom of heaven is likened unto a man which sowed good seed in his field: 25 But while men slept, his enemy came and sowed tares among the wheat, and went his way. 26 But when the blade was sprung up, and brought forth fruit, then appeared the tares also. 27 So the servants of the householder came and said unto him, Sir, didst not thou sow good seed in thy field? from whence then hath it tares? 28 He said unto them, An enemy hath done this. The servants said unto him, Wilt thou then that we go and gather them up? 29 But he said, Nay; lest while ye gather up the tares, ye root up also the wheat with them. 30 Let both grow together until the harvest: and in the time of harvest I will say to the reapers, Gather ye together first the tares, and bind them in bundles to burn them: but gather the wheat into my barn.

The enemy is constantly attempting to place divine similarities before us, just as the tares were set to supplant the wheat in Christ parabolic articulation. The spiritual duality is consistently present within our lives, whereby difficult choices must be made – often discerning ever so slight differences. Wheat and tares seem very similar, but the end product is vastly different. We must remain vigilantly focused, as we recognize that the wheat shall be bundled while the tares shall be burned. Prophetically proceeding through the process of life, helps us to embrace our sustaining Savior as gripping grace grows us through motivating mercy.

We must stay alert to God's will and way – not necessarily watching out for satan – but following God so closely that there is not opportunity for satanic leadership. Anytime we take our focus off of the Lord, there is an opportunity for satanic forces to capture our attention. It is virtually impossible for us to examine all of the counterfeits that will be presented to us. Nevertheless there is only one true God – therefore if we consistently focus on the truth, the lie automatically becomes marginal; and we will become hypersensitive to distracting deceptions.

David was instructed to purchase a threshing floor from Ornan the Jebusite and erect an altar on the threshing floor. Although Ornan was willing to give King David the property, the King refused the gift and insisted on paying the full price for the threshing floor. I wish we would embrace David's actions and recognize that we need to contribute/sacrifice – I know we find joy in the fact that Christ was sacrificed for us; but we should be so gratefully motivated to offer our all upon God's altar.

Worship requires our sacrifice, we must be willing to surrender to God our will, we must be willing to pay our all and stop shouting on credit! We can't be half saved; when we come to the altar we should be willing to bring our all. We should not habitually leave our perversion and profanity just long enough to stop by the church and read a few verses on Sunday, only to return to transgression - moments after worship. We should come through the door with our all, proclaiming that God may have our all, as we need the Lord and the power of salvation

Giving our all is often difficult, especially during those times when public repentance is required for our open transgressions – but the cost of restoration is well worth it. Many of us need to open our eyes to the mess that we have brought into the lives of others, and humble ourselves enough to go and offer apologies. There are parents that need to go to their children and apologies for living as hypocrites before them; some of our children are all messed up – because we taught them to be a mess! It is time for us to pay the full price and release our pride in order to embrace the consequential cost of our transgressions, the full price of restoration.

2 Chronicles 3:1-17 Then Solomon began to build the house of the LORD at Jerusalem in mount Moriah, where the LORD appeared unto David his father, in the place that David had prepared in the threshingfloor of Ornan the Jebusite. 2 And he began to build in the second day of the second month, in the fourth year of his reign. 3 Now these are the things wherein Solomon was instructed for the building of the house of God. The length by cubits after the first measure was threescore cubits, and the breadth twenty cubits. 4 And the porch that was in the front of the house, the length of it was according to the breadth of the house, twenty cubits, and the height was an hundred and twenty: and he overlaid it within with pure gold. 5 And the greater house he cieled with fir tree, which he overlaid with fine gold, and set thereon palm trees and chains. 6 And he garnished the house with precious stones for beauty: and the gold was gold of Parvaim. 7 He overlaid also the house, the beams, the posts, and the walls thereof, and the doors thereof, with gold; and graved cherubims on the walls. 8 And he made the most holy house, the length whereof was according to the breadth of the house, twenty cubits, and the breadth thereof twenty cubits: and he overlaid it with fine gold, amounting to six hundred talents. 9 And the weight of the nails was fifty shekels of gold. And he overlaid the upper chambers with gold. 10 And in the most holy house he made two cherubims of image work, and overlaid them with gold. 11 And the wings of the cherubims were twenty cubits long: one wing of the one cherub was five cubits, reaching to the wall of the house: and the other wing was likewise five cubits, reaching to the wing of the other cherub. 12 And one wing of the other cherub was five cubits, reaching to the wall of the house: and

50

the other wing was five cubits also, joining to the wing of the other cherub. 13 The wings of these cherubims spread themselves forth twenty cubits: and they stood on their feet, and their faces were inward. 14 And he made the vail of blue, and purple, and crimson, and fine linen, and wrought cherubims thereon. 15 Also he made before the house two pillars of thirty and five cubits high, and the chapiter that was on the top of each of them was five cubits. 16 And he made chains, as in the oracle, and put them on the heads of the pillars; and made an hundred pomegranates, and put them on the chains. 17 And he reared up the pillars before the temple, one on the right hand, and the other on the left; and called the name of that on the right hand Jachin, and the name of that on the left Boaz.

David built an altar on the threshing floor, which stands within the foreshadow of the building of the temple in 2 Chronicles 3:1 within the same region whereby Abraham had offered Isaac as a sacrifice years before on Mount Moriah (Genesis 22:2[17]). God works in a pattern, the same

---

[17] *Genesis 22:2   And he said, Take now thy son, thine only son Isaac, whom thou lovest, and get thee into the land of Moriah; and offer him there for a burnt offering upon one of the mountains which I will tell thee of.*

place where David had built an altar, his son Solomon builds the temple. The permanent sanctuary of God, the place of connection and meeting was erected upon the history of a threshing floor altar – a place steeped in the symbolic pattern of separation.

We should come to the altar of the Lord ready for separation. The separation took place in the mountain – our mindset should be lifted in the presence of God, we should come to the Lord recognizing that we are privileged to meet on the mount and not in the valley. God is ever present, yet the scriptures teach us that He dwells in a high place – the God that we worship, should motivate us to look up and think up – come into the courts of the Lord with praise and thanksgiving. The threshing floor reminds us not only that we should think on higher things, but we should be open to the wind – which represents the presence of God. John 3:5-8 illustrate that the wind process is so important to our transformation. God is like the wind, if you ask me how I know that God exists – I will ask you how do you know that the wind exists? What color is the wind? Where does the wind come from? Can you capture the wind? The wind is omnipresent, and powerful enough to wipe away entire cities, but gentle enough to cool us on a hot summer day. God is like the wind!

Now, let us remember that Moses had been instructed to build a tabernacle, with collected resources from the people. The place of worship that Moses was instructed to build was essentially a grand tent that would be erected within the center of the Israelite camp as they moved from place to place. It was a mobile place of worship, it was a mobile place of sacrifice, it was a mobile reminder that God was with them. The tabernacle was always at the center of the camp so that everyone could see it, at the center so that the people were continually motivated to acknowledge the prodigious purpose of life. Everywhere they went they took this tent with them, they would take it down, and put it back up the same way each time they moved.

In Chronicles we see that God instructs them to make a permanent place of worship. God's pattern can be seen in this transformation, as we are taught the divine process of God. When we accept the gift of salvation it takes time through God's process for us to arrive at a permanent place with the Lord, just as the Israelites went through trials and tribulations, so are we – moving from a nomadic relationship with the Lord, to a permanent place of worship. We should remember that God should be with us as we move throughout life, and ultimately we should seek to be firmly fixed toward the way of God's pattern. All of us have been at a level where we were transporting our worship, but lacked a permanent place for God in our life – thank God for grace that gives us the strength to continually build toward a permanent and fixed relationship with God. Grace provides us with the opportunity to keep growing toward God's pattern – we are moving toward the Lord's perfect way. Although we have not completely reached God's perfect way, we can keep reaching, and keep trying – as we see the Lord's tent in the midst of our camp, the tent of God in our business, the tent in our family, the Lord's tent in our finances; the great tent at the center of all that we do; leading us toward a daily relationship with God – firm and unmovable upon a mountain that is fixed.

The pattern helps us to stay the course in weak moments, just knowing all that the Lord has done to bring us to this day – knowing that I don't have to be perfect to come to Him; I merely need to start with a genuine relationship. Knowing that even in Adam and Eve's indiscretion He clothed them, knowing that He shared the pattern with Abraham and Isaac on a hill of decision as God provided the sacrifice, knowing that He shows us the pattern on the threshing floor with David – just knowing that the tent has laid the foundation for the temple stately proclaiming the presence of the Lord on Mt. Zion as a permanent proclamation that my Savior lives. David's story reminds us that our temple is built as a result of our repentance, and we are more than overcomers.

> Psalms 1:1-6 Blessed is the man that walketh not in the counsel of the ungodly, nor standeth in the way of sinners, nor sitteth in the seat of the scornful. 2 But his delight is in the law of the LORD; and in his law doth he meditate day and night. 3 And he shall be like a tree planted by the rivers of water, that bringeth forth his fruit in his season; his leaf also shall not wither; and whatsoever he doeth shall prosper. 4 The ungodly are not so: but are like the chaff which the wind driveth away. 5 Therefore the ungodly shall not stand in the judgment, nor sinners in the congregation of the righteous. 6 For the LORD knoweth the way of the righteous: but the way of the ungodly shall perish.

Let's go back and further understand the significance of the threshing floor. Psalm 1 illustrates for us the process by which the chaff is driven away by the wind – remember the threshing floor was a place of separation. The husk or the chaff was lifted off of the grain as the farmer would toss it into the air. The good grain would fall at the farmer's feet and the husk would be carried off by the wind. Notice that the grain does not grow up (perfect) without the chaff or husk, but through the farmer's process with the wind's influence – the good is separated from the bad. The useful from the useless – we are born with some stuff that needs to be separated.

We've been brought up in the dirt; we've been brought up in the husk. But the Holy Spirit, like the wind works in our life to separate or sanctify us. In Hebrews 4:12[18] we can see that God's word is like a sword that is able to bring separation into our life. Remember that when David purchased the threshing floor, he saw God above him with a sword in His hand. A relationship with God is not always comfortable, but forever profitable – when we come into the sanctuary of God we should be prepared for separation. Not separation from each other, but separation from sin.

---

[18] *Hebrews 4:12 For the word of God is quick, and powerful, and sharper than any twoedged sword, piercing even to the dividing asunder of soul and spirit, and of the joints and marrow, and is a discerner of the thoughts and intents of the heart.*

DIRT DIGGING:

LOOKING DEEPER

Genesis 2:7[19] reminds us that we have been created from the dust. Our connection with the dirt, seems fundamental to our faith journey. When we retain that we were created from dust, there are dormant functions that we may activate. Most life forms are dependent upon the health of the soil – the whole farm dies if the crops fail to flourish from the dirt. The earth is more than alive as the eco-system seems to emerge from the intimacy of soil and seed.

Revelation 12:1-17 And there appeared a great wonder in heaven; a woman clothed with the sun, and the moon under her feet, and upon her head a crown of twelve stars: 2 And she being with child cried, travailing in birth, and pained to be delivered. 3 And there appeared another wonder in heaven; and behold a great red dragon, having seven heads and ten horns, and seven crowns upon his heads. 4 And his

---

[19] *Genesis 2:7 And the LORD God formed man of the dust of the ground, and breathed into his nostrils the breath of life; and man became a living soul.*

tail drew the third part of the stars of heaven, and did cast them to the earth: and the dragon stood before the woman which was ready to be delivered, for to devour her child as soon as it was born. 5 And she brought forth a man child, who was to rule all nations with a rod of iron: and her child was caught up unto God, and to his throne. 6 And the woman fled into the wilderness, where she hath a place prepared of God, that they should feed her there a thousand two hundred and threescore days. 7 And there was war in heaven: Michael and his angels fought against the dragon; and the dragon fought and his angels, 8 And prevailed not; neither was their place found any more in heaven. 9 And the great dragon was cast out, that old serpent, called the Devil, and Satan, which deceiveth the whole world: he was cast out into the earth, and his angels were cast out with him. 10 And I heard a loud voice saying in heaven, Now is come salvation, and strength, and the kingdom of our God, and the power of his Christ: for the accuser of our brethren is cast down, which accused them before our God day and night. 11 And they overcame him by the blood of the Lamb, and by the word of their testimony; and they loved not their lives unto the death. 12 Therefore rejoice, ye heavens, and ye that dwell in them. Woe to the inhabiters of the earth and of the sea! for the devil is come down unto you, having great wrath, because he knoweth that he hath but a short time. 13 And when the dragon saw that he was cast unto the earth, he persecuted the woman which brought forth the man child. 14 And to the woman were given two wings of a great

62

eagle, that she might fly into the wilderness, into her place, where she is nourished for a time, and times, and half a time, from the face of the serpent. 15 And the serpent cast out of his mouth water as a flood after the woman, that he might cause her to be carried away of the flood. 16 And the earth helped the woman, and the earth opened her mouth, and swallowed up the flood which the dragon cast out of his mouth. 17 And the dragon was wroth with the woman, and went to make war with the remnant of her seed, which keep the commandments of God, and have the testimony of Jesus Christ.

In Revelation chapter 12 we see a beast depicted as a dragon with seven heads and ten horns – there is ugliness in the air through this symbol of satan. The early part of this chapter describes the dragon, and the later part of the chapter informs us that the dragon has purposed to pursue a woman and her child. The woman, seemingly symbolic of the twelve tribes of Israel and the church, containing the gift of Christ in her womb. The chapter tells us that the dragon is awaiting the birth of the baby, in order to destroy the infant. God protects the baby from the dragon, by having the baby brought to Heaven immediately after the birth. The dragon becomes mad with the woman, and decides to try to capture and kill her – after failing to fulfill destructive desires; the dragon wages war on the remnant of her commandment keeping seed. It seems important that we gain understanding around the importance of seed, as it relates to our future as Christians – blessing us with prophetic foundation that undergirds victorious triumph over satanic sustain. If the seed fails to flourish, then the threshing floor will remain desolate.

Seed is very important within the paradigm of the scriptures, in Genesis 2:7[20] we are told that

---

[20] *Genesis 2:7 And the LORD God formed man of the dust of the ground, and breathed into his nostrils the breath of life; and man became a living soul.*

64

man was created by the dust of the ground (dry dirt). Think about it, dirt is needed to plant seed (pre-scientific mutated modification and hydroponic discovery) and we are created from the dirt – therefore perfect for seed. It seems that we are both dirt and seed, inextricably bound through divine design. Within the etymological foundation of the word seed within a number of NT Biblical passage, our English word seed is translated from a root word most similar to our modern word sperm. In Ancient Hebrew the word seed is often transliterated *zera* or even older text may associate seed with the transliteration *ner* which means to "bring light" as well as a "newly plowed dirt" because plowing is seen as " bringing light to the soil", to the ancient Hebrew. In order for a seed to germinate, water must be present within the soil. When the ground is plowed the deeper dank soil surfaces and shines from the water in the soil which indicates that the water of life is present. Remember, that early on in a previous chapter we examined the similarities between creation and human copulation (merging light and waters to create matter). It seems to me that seed represent a viable part within God's paradigmatic parchment postulated toward the Lord's people.

It seems that the Lord was in fact leading us to learning when Adam was initially cursed to work agriculturally – perhaps this was the Lord's way of allowing Adam to count his blessing, perpetually discovering the ground from which he had been sculpted from its driest factions. Additionally, this should have been a humbling experience for Adam, as he was having to gain his sustaining substance from the seemingly lesser soil that he came from. Just think, he has been sculpted by God from the dirt, and now he had to depend on the dirt to feed his family. Oftentimes we forget where we come from, and begin to embrace illusions of grandeur – some of us need to look around and realize that we are nothing but dirt in shirts and britches.

Through the challenges of farming, we should recognize the parallels that emerge from the elements of the process. Seed are given spiritual value early on within the scriptures, as in Genesis 3:15[21] God curses the serpent, placing enmity between him and the seed of humankind.

---

[21] *Genesis 3:15 And I will put enmity between thee and the woman, and between thy seed and her seed; it shall bruise thy head, and thou shalt bruise his heel.*

In Revelation 12 after a long journey through time, we witness that the tension between satan and the seed remains constant throughout the Biblical paradigm. The satanic focus seems largely centralized around the seemingly weak yet powerfully potential stage of the seed. Adam and Eve had two sons (their seed) and one murdered the other. Abraham was desirous of a child, yet the seed did not manifest maturely for nearly the first century of his life. Abraham's son Isaac and his wife, had difficulty with conception – ultimately they had to petition God to bless them to conceive. Furthermore, Jacob was able to father many children through polygamy – yet he had difficulty impregnating Rachel (the woman he had struggled to marry). The old adversary is not primarily focused on your past or present – he desires to destroy your future! We must embrace the truth, that God alone has the power to protect, promote, and preserve our future.

Genesis 38:9[22] allows us to gain further evidence that God wants us to value our seed, as Onan seemingly angers the Lord by spilling his seed (sperm) on the ground as an intended method of birth control. I would submit to you that we must value the seed – Genesis 8:22[23] reminds us that seedtime and harvest is a constant principle of life that will remain as long as the earth is present. The paradigm of production is more than visible as we look at the seasons of environmental earth. God has created the wonders of the physical world as our classroom to apply the associative manifestations

---

[22] *Genesis 38:9 And Onan knew that the seed should not be his; and it came to pass, when he went in unto his brother's wife, that he spilled it on the ground, lest that he should give seed to his brother.*

[23] *Genesis 8:22 While the earth remaineth, seedtime and harvest, and cold and heat, and summer and winter, and day and night shall not cease.*

of the nonmaterial spiritual world – where things appear that are not seen.

Christ presents a number of parables surrounding agricultural terms. The parable of the seed and the sower, allow us to see the eschatological event of harvest – some seed will germinate beneficially toward a Heavenly eternity, and others will be lost to the abyss of destruction. Christ even presents the analogy of harvest and labor toward the spread of the Gospel and work of the disciple. The harvest is truly plentiful, yet the laborers are few – we need more Christians who value the agricultural plan of discipleship.

The seed alone is not enough, without a proper host and nurture, seeds left alone will not germinate through maturity. Psalm 1 reminds us that a blessed man meditating on the word of God in both day and night is like a tree that is planted by the rivers of water that bring forth fruit in the right season. We should not just be comfortable with the potential within seed; it should be our desire to become mature and fruitful. In Mathew chapter 21 we see the disdain of Christ with regards to a fig tree that was bare of fruit - leaves alone present no concrete evidence of our specific type. Although we may assume that a tree is an apple tree, we cannot be completely certain of the specific type, until fruit is produced.

The paradigm of the seed within the scriptures becomes important, because the requirement of sacrifice all starts with a seed.

Even in the case of animal sacrifice, seed had to be planted in order to produce sustenance for livestock. In the case of Cain and Able in Genesis 4:1-8[i] their sacrifices were not equally accepted by God and we are not completely certain as to why. Although a variety of commentaries have presented varied theses – upon summary conclusion God alone knows. 1Peter 1:21-25[ii] suggest that we must be reborn again by the word of God, becoming incorruptible seed. The word of God seems to emerge as a key factor within the transformation of seed.

The Gospel of John 1:1 states that: "In the beginning was the Word, and the Word was with God, and the Word was God," which seemingly attributes seed like characteristics to the word of

God which is also God. It seems mysterious for me, until the subsequent verse:

> John 1:1-14 In the beginning was the Word, and the Word was with God, and the Word was God. 2 The same was in the beginning with God. 3 All things were made by him; and without him was not any thing made that was made. 4 In him was life; and the life was the light of men. 5 And the light shineth in darkness; and the darkness comprehended it not. 6 There was a man sent from God, whose name was John. 7 The same came for a witness, to bear witness of the Light, that all men through him might believe. 8 He was not that Light, but was sent to bear witness of that Light. 9 That was the true Light, which lighteth every man that cometh into the world. 10 He was in the world, and the world was made by him, and the world knew him not. 11 He came unto his own, and his own received him not. 12 But as many as received him, to them gave he power to become the sons of God, even to them that believe on his name: 13 Which were born, not of blood, nor of the will of the flesh, nor of the will of man, but of God. 14 And the Word was made flesh, and dwelt among us, (and we beheld his glory, the glory as of the only begotten of the Father,) full of grace and truth.

In the beginning God created the heaven and the earth – the Spirit of God moved across face of the deep, and presented light, similarly classical human copulation contains comparable elements, as a man moves across a dark abyss to bring light to the waters. Remember that in some Ancient Hebrew text that seed relates to plowing which is etymologically connected to bringing light – acknowledging among other things that light is essential for growth. The first few chapters of John seem to contain two major elements within the early stages of germination – seed and light. Thinking upon the many passages related to seed, Revelation 22:13[24] the last passage within the printed Biblical text becomes clearer within our limited human interpretative intellectual

---

[24] *Revelation 22:13 I am Alpha and Omega, the beginning and the end, the first and the last.*

ideas – I've often ask how can you be the beginning and the end? How do you become your required sacrifice? Wondering how does God exist as God and become God at the same time – it seems easy when we think of seed (now faith is still required), as a seed starts a tree, and at the end of the process a seed is presented through the fruit. A seed is the beginning and the end – the word was there in the beginning (John 1:1) and endureth for ever (1Peter 1:25[25]). Finally we see the seed paradigm in the Gospel of Christ, as He (2Timothy 2:8[26]) was crucified, buried (planted), and arose on the third day – just as a germinated (matured) plant. We are but seeds with potential that can be manifested only

---

[25] *1 Peter 1:25 But the word of the Lord endureth for ever. And this is the word which by the gospel is preached unto you.*

[26] *2 Timothy 2:8 Remember that Jesus Christ of the seed of David was raised from the dead according to my gospel:*

through Christ - Philippians 3:10-11 says: "That I may know him, and the power of his resurrection, and the fellowship of his sufferings, being made conformable unto his death; If by any means I might attain unto the resurrection of the dead." Our potential is released through our connection with Christ. We cannot afford to ignore the pattern of God as our growth is more than dependent on remaining in the right soil, nurtured by the waters of the Holy Spirit, and light of the Lord.

TWO SIDES, YOU CHOOSE,

ONE PURPOSE

The fall of humankind in the garden creates a pattern that makes a duality necessary for redemption. Think of the duality as an event followed by an apology, or a spill followed by a cleanup - 1 Corinthians 15:22 states that "For as in Adam all die, even so in Christ shall all be made alive". We often embrace that notion that Christ is the only son of God, however the scriptures teach us in Luke 3:1[27] that Adam was also the son of God. Adam was the created son of God and Christ was the born son of God. Adam was the older brother that brought death, and Christ the younger brother that brought life. Between the age of Adam and the time of Christ, the scriptures present this paradigm of

---

[27] *Luke 3:1 Now in the fifteenth year of the reign of Tiberius Caesar, Pontius Pilate being governor of Judaea, and Herod being tetrarch of Galilee, and his brother Philip tetrarch of Ituraea and of the region of Trachonitis, and Lysanias the tetrarch of Abilene,*

redemption many times. Cain and Abel were the first hint of this pre-formation that lead us to a host of others. Research teaches us that Abram (later renamed Abraham) was the younger brother from his family, yet his name appears first within the scriptures because he was given the promise of God.

The dual list is long leading us and teaching us toward Christ. Just to name a few of the scriptural redemptive patterned foreshadows:

1. Abraham had two sons, Ishmael and Isaac (1 Chronicles 1:28[28]).

---

[28] *1 Chronicles 1:28 The sons of Abraham; Isaac, and Ishmael.*

2. Abraham was directed to sacrifice his son, yet a ram was substituted by God (Genesis 22:13[29]).

3. Isaac had Esau and Jacob (Genesis 25:26[30]).

4. Jacob's first born son Reuben was bypassed and his inheritance was given to his brother Judah, because Reuben had slept with one of his father's wives. Additionally, Jacob had two sets of children, and the first of the second set was Joseph – who was used by

---

[29] *Genesis 22:13 And Abraham lifted up his eyes, and looked, and behold behind him a ram caught in a thicket by his horns: and Abraham went and took the ram, and offered him up for a burnt offering in the stead of his son.*

[30] *Genesis 25:26 And after that came his brother out, and his hand took hold on Esau's heel; and his name was called Jacob: and Isaac was threescore years old when she bare them.*

God to save the entire family from famine (Genesis 30:24[31]).

5. The Children of Israel had two life cycles, before the Red Sea and after Sinai (Numbers 3:1[32]).

6. Israel had two major cycles of leadership, the time of the Judges and the time of the Kings (2Kings 23:22[33]).

7. Two kings representing the competing forces of good and evil – David and Saul (1 Samuel 18:12[34]).

---

[31] *Genesis 30:24 And she called his name Joseph; and said, The LORD shall add to me another son.*

[32] *Numbers 3:1 These also are the generations of Aaron and Moses in the day that the LORD spake with Moses in mount Sinai.*

[33] *2 Kings 23:22 Surely there was not holden such a passover from the days of the judges that judged Israel, nor in all the days of the kings of Israel, nor of the kings of Judah;*

8. Joseph had two sons Ephraim and Manasseh (Genesis 46:20[35]).

The dual paradigm consistently implores us to embrace change within our own spiritual life. Nicodemus was told by Christ in John 3:3 that in order to see the Kingdom of God; rebirth is necessary. 1 Peter 1:23[36], teaches us that we have been wrought of corruptible seed, and we must be born again in order to emerge from incorruptible seed. God rejects the first creature created, and requires the redeemed creation born into His holy family.

---

[34] *1 Samuel 18:12 And Saul was afraid of David, because the LORD was with him, and was departed from Saul.*

[35] *Genesis 46:20 And unto Joseph in the land of Egypt were born Manasseh and Ephraim, which Asenath the daughter of Potipherah priest of On bare unto him.*

[36] *1 Peter 1:23 Being born again, not of corruptible seed, but of incorruptible, by the word of God, which liveth and abideth for ever.*

82

1 Corinthians 6:19[37] seems to teach us that our
bodies are not our own, but we are the temple of
the Holy Spirit – we have yet another kind of
duality, as we are blessed to represent both the
movable and transportable place of God
(Tabernacle), but at the same time the fixed and
permanent place of God (Temple) . Everywhere
we go God should be so much within us that the
presence of God should be permanently with us
throughout the Christian journey. As we enter
into tabernacle with the Holy Spirit, the mindset
of the threshing floor should be with us –
embracing the necessity to separate sin out of our
lives. In the season of Pentecost, there was a voice
like a mighty rushing wind – high upon the
mountain of God's word upon the establishment
of our Savior. If we but open the windows of our

---

[37] *1 Corinthians 6:19 What? know ye not that your body is the temple of the Holy
Ghost which is in you, which ye have of God, and ye are not your own?*

life to welcome the Holy Spirit to separate transgression from us, that we might worship the Lord our deliverer and savior. God cared enough about us that the sacrificial blood of Christ has been provided to eternally redeem us, rather than the limited sacrifice of lesser animals[38].

Although Christ sacrificed His life for us, we have a part within the process. Philippians 3:10[39] places us in relationship with the sacrifice and resurrection of our savior. Many modern preachers promulgate the idea of a prosperity gospel anchored upon a principle of seedtime and harvest (Genesis 8:22[40]). I would contend that it is imposable to please God without fully

---

[38] Hebrews 10:1-10

[39] *Philippians 3:10 That I may know him, and the power of his resurrection, and the fellowship of his sufferings, being made conformable unto his death;*

[40] *Genesis 8:22 While the earth remaineth, seedtime and harvest, and cold and heat, and summer and winter, and day and night shall not cease.*

embracing the final manifestation of harvest leading to the threshing floor and ultimately to the altar of sacrifice.

Leviticus provides the instructions for the five types of sacrifice, devoting the first five chapters to the sacred process. The burnt, meal, peace, sin, and trespass offerings – are all early patterns of Christ's salvific work.

The offerings followed a paradigm Christ fulfills in order to meet the requirements of God. Leviticus chapters 1-5 gives us a clear foreshadow of redemption as the burnt offering represents that all I am is Christ's, the grain offering proclaims that all I have is Christ's, the peace offering articulates that all my joy is in Christ, the sin and trespass offerings illustrate that all my salvation is in Christ. Jesus the Christ is the ultimate sacrifice satisfying the prerequisite of salvation upon the cross, fulfilling the requirements of the Levitical Law. Nevertheless, the five offerings also reveal different aspects of what we are, as fallen humans from the pattern of Adam. The Biblical paradigm seems to represent a repetitive refrain that beckons our attention toward the same message – we are not acceptable as created, God requires our birth into the Holy Family; and the proper paradigm must take place for conception. Leading us to remember the light discussed in previous chapters, presenting a consistent glimpse of God's pattern toward separation – inextricably bound to the growth process and the ideology of sanctification, even in as much as light notably denotes a separation from darkness.

WADING IN THE WATER

Jesus admonishes Nicodemus to be born again (John 3:1-23[iii]) through the water and Spirit – which provides sustaining revelation toward the 1Peter 1:23[41] passage that suggests we must be born again of incorruptible seed, by God's word. The waters of baptism seem to emerge early on within the Bible – the idea of redevelopment though separation, as God places boundaries within the elements presented in Genesis 1:1-10. Additionally, the idea of being redeveloped through purification may even be a part of Adam and Eve's back story. It would seem plausible that after the great fall, when God provided clothes for the shamed couple – the animal skin garments had to be fashioned through God's divine haberdashery. Certainly, if

---

[41] *1 Peter 1:23 Being born again, not of corruptible seed, but of incorruptible, by the word of God, which liveth and abideth for ever.*

we revisit creation in light of God's work – and the ability that humans are given to conceive; there is an element of water as we are all born physically dependent of oxygen, yet born of water.

The divine process of separation, known as sanctification was manifested as foreshadow in the life of Moses as his family places him in a basket floated upon the Nile River in order to redeem him from genocide. Moses was primarily separated from his camp, culture, and caste through a redemptive basket ride to safety. God used Moses' years after the Nile River (baptism) to lead refugees out of Egypt through the Red Sea – which seems like a mass baptism, symbolizing purifying separation from captive bondage through the power of God's hand of deliverance.

The baptism paradigm seems to flow throughout the scriptures, as we are privileged to witness through the passages the crafting of wash basins and the washing of ritual sacrifices (Leviticus 1:9[42] and 2Chronicles 4:6[43]).

The waters of separation are so profound to the Biblical pattern that even Christ (a perfect sacrifice) was baptized. Interestingly, the baptism of Christ was one of the few times that we concretely see the presence of the Father, Son, and Holy Spirit totally manifested within our human capacity to witness divine presence. The Baptism of Christ is one of the five major events

---

[42] *Leviticus 1:9 But his inwards and his legs shall he wash in water: and the priest shall burn all on the altar, to be a burnt sacrifice, an offering made by fire, of a sweet savour unto the LORD.*

[43] *2 Chronicles 4:6 He made also ten lavers, and put five on the right hand, and five on the left, to wash in them: such things as they offered for the burnt offering they washed in them; but the sea was for the priests to wash in.*

within the scriptural narrative of the Messiah, which all at once leads us to understand the fullness of physical and spiritual germination conjoined with the elements of sacrifice. Christ was baptized (watered), transfigured (transformed), crucified (harvested and lifted just as a Levitical sacrifice), (replanted) resurrected, and ascended (like smoke from the altar of burnt sacrifices). All of the Old Testament elements of redemption may be witnessed within the life of Christ, as he fulfills the divine pattern. Understanding the paradigm is important, as we must follow Christ through similar processes attempting to connect with Him in the fellowship of His sufferings and power of His resurrection[44].

---

[44] Philippians 3:9-11

A FEW LAST WORDS, WITH

A HINT OF BEFORE

It seems most appropriate that we conclude with the born son of God through the communion of the seed of David. Jesus is the product of God through 42 generations, revealing the redemptive power of God.

Christ's final words (known as the seven words or sayings) from Calvary seem to capture events from the journey of the Israelites during the exodus era. The ability to exit is just as important as knowing how to enter. We are frequently asking the Lord to open doors and new opportunities, yet far too often we are not prepared to leave the past behind.

Christ demonstrates that there will be times when an exit may be profoundly more traumatic than an entrance – but necessary to complete an assignment. Seemingly the Israelites may testify also, as they were received by the Egyptians with hospitality – but decades later their exit came with great struggle. Similarities between the Calvary conversation and the Exodus from Egypt seem to present an exit paradigm.

I. Word of Forgiveness

Christ says "forgive them" (Luke 23:34[45]) –
Pharaoh ask for forgiveness (Exodus 10:16[46]) and
Moses intercedes for the Israelites to gain
forgiveness (Numbers 14:19[47]). Forgiveness
emerges early on within the Biblical narrative
through God's grace and mercy extended to
Adam.

The Lord has extended forgiveness to
humanity many times, from the society of Noah
to our modern period. Christ reminds us in the

---

[45] *Luke 23:34 Then said Jesus, Father, forgive them; for they know not what they do. And they parted his raiment, and cast lots.*

[46] *Exodus 10:16 Then Pharaoh called for Moses and Aaron in haste; and he said, I have sinned against the LORD your God, and against you.*

[47] *Numbers 14:19 Pardon, I beseech thee, the iniquity of this people according unto the greatness of thy mercy, and as thou hast forgiven this people, from Egypt even until now.*

model prayer (Matthew 6:12[48]) that we must forgive as we expect to be forgiven. The principle of forgiveness is a key component to a healthy life – as unforgiveness is like a cancer that infects positive progress. Our ability to forgive is a manifestation of our faith, showing that we trust God to bring forth good (Romans 8:28[49]) within our life even when evil seems immanent. We must trust that God will bless us in spite of adversity, for the Lord declares that vengeance (Romans 12:19[50]) must not be a part of our actions. Our trust must always remain in God's ability to protect us in every way; therefore we will find it easier to forgive, as we become

---

[48] *Matthew 6:12 And forgive us our debts, as we forgive our debtors.*

[49] *Romans 8:28 And we know that all things work together for good to them that love God, to them who are the called according to his purpose.*

[50] *Romans 12:19 Dearly beloved, avenge not yourselves, but rather give place unto wrath: for it is written, Vengeance is mine; I will repay, saith the Lord.*

stronger in faith. People can hurt us only if we misdirect our attention away from God.

It seems that the ultimate lesson on forgiveness is taught upon the cross of Calvary – as Christ intercedes for humanity through word and deed. Although the totality of the cross is a testimony of perfected work, the words "forgive them" should continue to ring loud within the heart of every Christian, prompting compassionate declarations of love; manifested through action. Ultimately, unforgiveness is a result of a bad memory – who among us is great enough to surpass the need for forgiveness? I am reminded of Christ in John 8, when an adulterous woman tagged for capital punishment was brought to Him; and He responded with the phrase "He that is without sin among you, let him first cast a stone at her". If we look back over our life and think about the many times that we have been forgiven – then we should release our stones and be quick to embrace the regenerative treasure of love.

Moses as a prefiguration of Christ intercedes for the Children of Israel – as God was ready to destroy them. Moses maintains the heart of a leader for the people. Christians are designed to forgive; it is our duty to restore those who have been overtaken with a fault (Galatians 6:1[51]). Famously, Christ admonishes humankind to turn the other check (Matthew 5:38-40[52]), when asked

---

[51] *Galatians 6:1   Brethren, if a man be overtaken in a fault, ye which are spiritual, restore such an one in the spirit of meekness; considering thyself, lest thou also be tempted.*

[52] *Matthew 5:38-40   Ye have heard that it hath been said, An eye for an eye, and a tooth for a tooth: 39   But I say unto you, That ye resist not evil: but whosoever shall*

how often we should forgive – Christ presents a number that suggests continual forgiveness (Matthew 18:22[53], Luke 17:4[54]).

---

smite thee on thy right cheek, turn to him the other also. 40 And if any man will sue thee at the law, and take away thy coat, let him have thy cloke also.

[53] Matthew 18:22 Jesus saith unto him, I say not unto thee, Until seven times: but, Until seventy times seven.

[54] Luke 17:4 And if he trespass against thee seven times in a day, and seven times in a day turn again to thee, saying, I repent; thou shalt forgive him.

II. Word of Salvation

Christ provides hope to the thief on the cross, proclaiming "today you will be with me in paradise" (Luke 23:43[55]) – the children of Israel depart from Egypt with a mixed multitude (Exodus 12:38[56]).

Adam and Eve were saved from themselves and their nakedness was covered by our merciful God. Surely the Adam family would have been lost had the Lord not intervened. It seems that one of the main points of the scriptures directs us to understand that when left to ourselves –

---

[55] Luke 23:43 And Jesus said unto him, Verily I say unto thee, To day shalt thou be with me in paradise.

[56] Exodus 12:38 And a mixed multitude went up also with them; and flocks, and herds, even very much cattle.

destruction is forthwith. The Bible warns us not to trust our innate intuition (Isaiah 5:21[57], Proverbs 3:5[58]) – our constant faith must remain in the salvific power of God. Christ is the same yesterday, today, and forevermore (Hebrews 13:8[59]) – providing us with perpetual hope to life through communion with His great sacrifice. Although we were all lost through the one man Adam – we are all saved through the one man Christ (Romans 5:19[60]).

We should be eternally grateful, hearts filled with worship, as we have been bought with a

---

[57] *Isaiah 5:21 Woe unto them that are wise in their own eyes, and prudent in their own sight!*

[58] *Proverbs 3:5 Trust in the LORD with all thine heart; and lean not unto thine own understanding.*

[59] *Hebrews 13:8 Jesus Christ the same yesterday, and to day, and for ever.*

[60] *Romans 5:19 For as by one man's disobedience many were made sinners, so by the obedience of one shall many be made righteous.*

price – the precious life of the Messiah (1Corinthians 6:20[61]). The shadow of the sacrifice can be seen through the relationship between Abraham and his son Isaac as God steps in and provides the sacrifice in the bush. The regeneration of our salvation is evident through the deliverance of the Israelites from Pharaoh's wickedness in Egypt. The Lord is strong and mighty in power time and time again throughout the scriptures saving us by various means – "for there is no restraint to the Lord to save by many or by few" (1Samual 14:6[62]). Hallelujah, our God is King of Kings and Lord of Lords!

---

[61] *1 Corinthians 6:20 For ye are bought with a price: therefore glorify God in your body, and in your spirit, which are God's.*

[62] *1 Samuel 14:6 And Jonathan said to the young man that bare his armour, Come, and let us go over unto the garrison of these uncircumcised: it may be that the LORD will work for us: for there is no restraint to the LORD to save by many or by few.*

The thief on the cross provides hope for us that it is never too late to receive Christ, yet there is a limit to grace as judgment day shall come. We are not told the lineage of the thief on the cross, his socio-economic status is not known – but his destination was clearly pronounced. Christ has commanded us to love one another, commissioning us to teach and baptize all nations. Isolation of race, nationality, and status works against the mandate of the Great Commission. History articulates that when the Israelites departed from Egypt, they were a mixed multitude. The church would be so beautiful, if the people of God would embrace the divine ideology of a mixed tribe teaching and baptizing all nations.

III. Word of Relationship

Christ focuses on his mother with the words "behold my mother" (John 19:26-27[63]) – the Israelites take the bones of their forefather Joseph through the Red Sea away from Egypt (Genesis 50:25[64], Exodus 13:19[65]).

The family seems to be God's portrait of what healthy life should look like. From the very beginning, God created family as a gift to humanity. Adam was lonely; therefore God presented him with the gift of family. The scripture articulates that a wife is good – further

---

[63] *John 19:26-27 When Jesus therefore saw his mother, and the disciple standing by, whom he loved, he saith unto his mother, Woman, behold thy son! 27 Then saith he to the disciple, Behold thy mother! And from that hour that disciple took her unto his own home.*

[64] *Genesis 50:25 And Joseph took an oath of the children of Israel, saying, God will surely visit you, and ye shall carry up my bones from hence.*

[65] *Exodus 13:19 And Moses took the bones of Joseph with him: for he had straitly sworn the children of Israel, saying, God will surely visit you; and ye shall carry up my bones away hence with you.*

strengthening the value of familial relationships (Proverbs 18:22[66]). The epistle to the Ephesians articulates relative themes around family and the church – illustrating the importance of relationships (Ephesians 5:25[67]).

Think about it, all of the fathers of faith were married with children within the early history of the Biblical narrative. Furthermore, from the era of Abraham to the era of the Promised Land, the families were nomadic and isolation would have been fatal.

Although the Son of God could have been presented in a number of ways – Christ was

---

[66] *Proverbs 18:22 Whoso findeth a wife findeth a good thing, and obtaineth favour of the LORD.*

[67] *Ephesians 5:25 Husbands, love your wives, even as Christ also loved the church, and gave himself for it;*

delivered through a familial relationship. God so loved the world that we have been given the gift of Christ wrapped in the splendor of connective communion. The family is a resource for each of us to understand the divine creative movement that comes from God to build rather than destroy.

Within the Decalogue (commonly referred to as the Ten Commandments) God mandates the honorable treatment of one's father and mother, adding a promise of long life to the adherent. Christ demonstrates His devotion to the divine law, even with the pangs of the crucifixion – He stops to focus on His mother. Similarly the children of Israel were hurriedly departing from Egypt with predators in pursuit – but they remembered the bones of Joseph. Around two centuries after the death of Joseph – they honored his request to be posthumously   removed from the land of bondage. Biblically, family maintains the kind of importance that is not even diminished by agony and death. It seems to me that the family is a primary resource toward understanding the divine pattern. Many passages in the Biblical text parallel the earthly family structure with the celestial pattern of God. We are physically here as a result of the light emerging from our parents copulation – we remain spiritually viable as a result of the light that God provides to lead us from darkness to eternal reward. The great Creator united the family within a parallel existence necessary for eternal optimization.

IV. Word of Abandonment

Christ utters a word of abandonment, "Eli, Eli, lama sabachthani? that is to say, My God, my God, why hast thou forsaken me?" (Matthew 27:46[68], Mark 15:34[69]) – the Israelites complain that God and Moses had brought them to the wilderness to die (Numbers 21:4-5[70]).

During the crucifixion of Christ, He took on the sins of humanity through the sadness of a forsaken period. The holy attribute of God the

---

[68] *Matthew 27:46   And about the ninth hour Jesus cried with a loud voice, saying, Eli, Eli, lama sabachthani? that is to say, My God, my God, why hast thou forsaken me?*

[69] *Mark 15:34   And at the ninth hour Jesus cried with a loud voice, saying, Eloi, Eloi, lama sabachthani? which is, being interpreted, My God, my God, why hast thou forsaken me?*

[70] *Numbers 21:4-5   And they journeyed from mount Hor by the way of the Red sea, to compass the land of Edom: and the soul of the people was much discouraged because of the way.   5   And the people spake against God, and against Moses, Wherefore have ye brought us up out of Egypt to die in the wilderness? for there is no bread, neither is there any water; and our soul loatheth this light bread.*

Father had to turn from the cross during the Calvary context, as sin was extant. The Lord has continually maintained that sanctification is necessary for divine assembly with humanity – as God admonishes us to be holy (Leviticus 11:44[71]). God's light will not be diminished, to contain our darkness – therefore the Lord would rather turn from us than destroy us. The light emanating from the Lord would instantly consume us if God refused to turn from our sinful state.

God prepares us for traumatic seasons through the beauty of divine gleams during seasons of abandonment – even as the Lord turns, light may be seen by those diligently

---

[71] *Leviticus 11:44 For I am the LORD your God: ye shall therefore sanctify yourselves, and ye shall be holy; for I am holy: neither shall ye defile yourselves with any manner of creeping thing that creepeth upon the earth.*

seeking God. We have been wonderfully made (Psalms 139:14[72]), and provided with all of the resources needed to fight against the authorities of sin (Ephesians 6:10-18[iv]). Additionally, the Lord has given us a portrait of divine living – Adam and Eve were initially placed in a divinely sustained garden (Genesis 2:8[73]), the children of Israel were given a Promised Land prominent with milk and honey (Joshua 5:6[74]), we have been given access to Heaven (Matthew 6:10[75]) as we are also the temple of the Holy Spirit

---

[72] *Psalms 139:14 I will praise thee; for I am fearfully and wonderfully made: marvellous are thy works; and that my soul knoweth right well.*

[73] *Genesis 2:8 And the LORD God planted a garden eastward in Eden; and there he put the man whom he had formed.*

[74] *Joshua 5:6 For the children of Israel walked forty years in the wilderness, till all the people that were men of war, which came out of Egypt, were consumed, because they obeyed not the voice of the LORD: unto whom the LORD sware that he would not shew them the land, which the LORD sware unto their fathers that he would give us, a land that floweth with milk and honey.*

[75] *Matthew 6:10 Thy kingdom come. Thy will be done in earth, as it is in heaven.*

(1Corinthians 6:19[76]). God has shown us how it could be and should be – it is up to us to abandon the life of a run away and return home to our heavenly parent.

Each time that humankind has strayed away from God the natural consequential lessons that evolve should teach us that the agony of separation is not worth the fantasy of autonomy. Our greatest desire should continually exclaim words of worship and praise, offering our all to the God we love! Please God never leave us nor forsake us – for we need you in every part of our lives.

Although Christ utters word of abandonment because sacrifice led him to the corridor of

---

[76] *1 Corinthians 6:19 What? know ye not that your body is the temple of the Holy Ghost which is in you, which ye have of God, and ye are not your own?*

111

forsakenness – the Israelites felt abandoned because they did not trust God. The Lord is continually available, however we tend to complain when we cannot trace God – but we should trust the Lord even in times when visibility is dimly dark. The Lord has promised never to leave us – and if we but remember the great goodness of God, and all that has been done for us, we should never complain. If the Lord never does anything else for us – Calvary is proof, that enough has been done.

V. Word of Distress

Christ articulates a physical need stating, "I thirst" (John 19:28[77]) – the Israelites complain of thirst (Exodus 17:3[78]).

Most often we will find ourselves in a state of distress in the midst of a season of forsaken feelings, brought on by isolation. Christ voluntarily offered Himself as a sacrifice for us, as He relinquished His Heavenly power to rectify a mundane condition. God created us from the dust, allowing us to identify with the substandard reality of the material world. Our

---

[77] *John 19:28 After this, Jesus knowing that all things were now accomplished, that the scripture might be fulfilled, saith, I thirst.*

[78] *Exodus 17:3 And the people thirsted there for water; and the people murmured against Moses, and said, Wherefore is this that thou hast brought us up out of Egypt, to kill us and our children and our cattle with thirst?*

earthly journey seems to be a constant discovery of God's ultimate desire for us to live as spiritual constructions. The flesh seems to be the weight placed upon us to strengthen our spiritual reality.

When in distress we are often drawn toward physical needs just as we witness within the thirsty proclamation of Christ and the Israelites. The scriptures teach us that our fight is not against flesh and blood – but our fight is of a spiritual nature (Ephesians 6:12[79]). We must constantly remain aware that the forces of darkness are at work when our physical bodies become distractions (Romans 12:2[80]). Our journey toward death and physical decay are constant

---

[79] *Ephesians 6:12   For we wrestle not against flesh and blood, but against principalities, against powers, against the rulers of the darkness of this world, against spiritual wickedness in high places.*

[80] *Romans 12:2   And be not conformed to this world: but be ye transformed by the renewing of your mind, that ye may prove what is that good, and acceptable, and perfect, will of God.*

reminders that in Adam we all die – yet in Christ we all live, for the gift of God is eternal life (Romans 6:22-23[81], John 3:16[82]).

Although the cross was a perfected display of Christ humanity conjoined with divine humility – the endurance of our Savior remains within the fact that a deep fountain was flowing in spite of His physical thirst (John 4:14[83]). When we are in communion with Christ, thirsty times will come – yet spiritual hydration will sustain us through any situation or dry season.

---

[81] Romans 6:22-23 But now being made free from sin, and become servants to God, ye have your fruit unto holiness, and the end everlasting life. 23 For the wages of sin is death; but the gift of God is eternal life through Jesus Christ our Lord.

[82] John 3:16 For God so loved the world, that he gave his only begotten Son, that whosoever believeth in him should not perish, but have everlasting life.

[83] John 4:14 But whosoever drinketh of the water that I shall give him shall never thirst; but the water that I shall give him shall be in him a well of water springing up into everlasting life.

God is super supreme and can create a way out of no way – where we cannot see the path the Lord has already prepared a way. The Lord is a rock in a weary land and water in dry places (Exodus 17:5-6[84]). The Lord is the great shepherd which leads us to the still waters to endure us – but we must embrace Jesus, the bread of life that promises that if we come to Him, we shall never hunger or thirst. Praise the Lord for divine protection and provision. The Lord watches over us both day and night – caring for us through various seasons.

---

[84] *Exodus 17:5-6 And the LORD said unto Moses, Go on before the people, and take with thee of the elders of Israel; and thy rod, wherewith thou smotest the river, take in thine hand, and go. 6 Behold, I will stand before thee there upon the rock in Horeb; and thou shalt smite the rock, and there shall come water out of it, that the people may drink. And Moses did so in the sight of the elders of Israel.*

VI. Word of Triumph

Christ declares "it is finished" (John 19:30[85]) –
the Israelites sang a song of triumph after
crossing the Red Sea to liberation (Exodus 15).
Moses dies before the children of Israel enter the
promise land (Deuteronomy 34:5[86]).

In the words of a song: "I'm so glad trouble
don't last always" – however the darkest part of
day comes before dawn. We must remain faithful
embracing hope through the realization that the
crucifixion came before the resurrection. Far too
often we drop out of the race set before us
because we become dependent on earthly
monikers of success – along with our strengths

---

[85] *John 19:30 When Jesus therefore had received the vinegar, he said, It is finished: and he bowed his head, and gave up the ghost.*

[86] *Deuteronomy 34:5 So Moses the servant of the LORD died there in the land of Moab, according to the word of the LORD.*

and ability (Ecclesiastes 9:11[87], Matthew 24:13[88], 2Timothy 4:7[89]). Our total dependence for triumph must be established upon the strength of our God.

- The Lord shall supply all of my needs (Philippians 4:19[90]).
- The Lord shall make my enemies my footstools (Matthew 22:44[91]).
- The Battle is the Lord's (2Chronicles 20:1-29[v], Psalm 24:8[92]).

---

[87] *Ecclesiastes 9:11 I returned, and saw under the sun, that the race is not to the swift, nor the battle to the strong, neither yet bread to the wise, nor yet riches to men of understanding, nor yet favour to men of skill; but time and chance happeneth to them all.*

[88] *Matthew 24:13 But he that shall endure unto the end, the same shall be saved.*

[89] *2 Timothy 4:7 I have fought a good fight, I have finished my course, I have kept the faith:*

[90] *Philippians 4:19 But my God shall supply all your need according to his riches in glory by Christ Jesus.*

[91] *Matthew 22:44 The LORD said unto my Lord, Sit thou on my right hand, till I make thine enemies thy footstool?*

[92] *Psalms 24:8 Who is this King of glory? The LORD strong and mighty, the LORD mighty in battle.*

- Death has been defeated (1Corinthians 15:55[93], Isaiah 25:8[94]).

- Christ emerged with power (Matthew 28:18[95])

- No weapon formed against us shall prosper (Isaiah 54:17[96]).

The Lord is in control, God formed the foundation of the earth before our arrival (Job 38:4[97]) and the earth belongs to the Lord along

---

[93] *1 Corinthians 15:55 O death, where is thy sting? O grave, where is thy victory?*

[94] *Isaiah 25:8 He will swallow up death in victory; and the Lord GOD will wipe away tears from off all faces; and the rebuke of his people shall he take away from off all the earth: for the LORD hath spoken it.*

[95] *Matthew 28:18 And Jesus came and spake unto them, saying, All power is given unto me in heaven and in earth.*

[96] *Isaiah 54:17 No weapon that is formed against thee shall prosper; and every tongue that shall rise against thee in judgment thou shalt condemn. This is the heritage of the servants of the LORD, and their righteousness is of me, saith the LORD.*

[97] *Job 38:4 Where wast thou when I laid the foundations of the earth? declare, if thou hast understanding.*

with all of its inhabitants (Psalm 24:1[98]). We must remember that the Lord loved us before there was a when or a where, our only task is to connect with the will and way of God (Proverbs 8:22-36[99]). God is in control of all that we see, know, or can imagine. Christ is both the beginning and the end – alpha and omega. Triumph has been established from the commencement of the world – our God is King!

---

[98] *Psalms 24:1 The earth is the LORD'S, and the fulness thereof; the world, and they that dwell therein.*

[99] *Proverbs 8:22-36 The LORD possessed me in the beginning of his way, before his works of old. 23 I was set up from everlasting, from the beginning, or ever the earth was. 24 When there were no depths, I was brought forth; when there were no fountains abounding with water. 25 Before the mountains were settled, before the hills was I brought forth: 26 While as yet he had not made the earth, nor the fields, nor the highest part of the dust of the world. 27 When he prepared the heavens, I was there: when he set a compass upon the face of the depth: 28 When he established the clouds above: when he strengthened the fountains of the deep: 29 When he gave to the sea his decree, that the waters should not pass his commandment: when he appointed the foundations of the earth: 30 Then I was by him, as one brought up with him: and I was daily his delight, rejoicing always before him; 31 Rejoicing in the habitable part of his earth; and my delights were with the sons of men. 32 Now therefore hearken unto me, O ye children: for blessed are they that keep my ways. 33 Hear instruction, and be wise, and refuse it not. 34 Blessed is the man that heareth me, watching daily at my gates, waiting at the posts of my doors. 35 For whoso findeth me findeth life, and shall obtain favour of the LORD. 36 But he that sinneth against me wrongeth his own soul: all they that hate me love death.*

VII. Word of Reunion

Christ says, "Father, into thy hands I commend my spirit" (Luke 23:46[100]) – God declared divine presence with the Israelites (Joshua 1:9[101]).

Just as the Prodigal awaited the return of his son (Luke 15:11-31[vi]) – God awaits our return. The Lord invites us to come from every perspective no matter the condition (Mathew 11:28[102]). We have strayed away from God, but all we must do is turn through repentance and Holy Spirit led living.

---

[100] *Luke 23:46 And when Jesus had cried with a loud voice, he said, Father, into thy hands I commend my spirit: and having said thus, he gave up the ghost.*

[101] *Joshua 1:9 Have not I commanded thee? Be strong and of a good courage; be not afraid, neither be thou dismayed: for the LORD thy God is with thee whithersoever thou goest.*

[102] *Matthew 11:28 Come unto me, all ye that labour and are heavy laden, and I will give you rest.*

[God] "I hope, by thy good pleasure, safely to arrive at home. Jesus sought me when a stranger, wandering from the fold of God; he, to rescue me from danger, interposed his precious blood. O to grace how great a debtor daily I'm constrained to be! Let thy goodness, like a fetter, bind my wandering heart to thee. Prone to wander, Lord, I feel it, prone to leave the God I love; here's my heart, O take and seal it, seal it for thy courts above! (Robert Robinson, 1757)

Some day we will make it home – home sweet home, where our God anticipates our return!

End Notes

ⁱ *Genesis 4:1-8 And Adam knew Eve his wife; and she conceived, and bare Cain, and said, I have gotten a man from the LORD. 2 And she again bare his brother Abel. And Abel was a keeper of sheep, but Cain was a tiller of the ground. 3 And in process of time it came to pass, that Cain brought of the fruit of the ground an offering unto the LORD. 4 And Abel, he also brought of the firstlings of his flock and of the fat thereof. And the LORD had respect unto Abel and to his offering: 5 But unto Cain and to his offering he had not respect. And Cain was very wroth, and his countenance fell. 6 And the LORD said unto Cain, Why art thou wroth? and why is thy countenance fallen? 7 If thou doest well, shalt thou not be accepted? and if thou doest not well, sin lieth at the door. And unto thee shall be his desire, and thou shalt rule over him. 8 And Cain talked with Abel his brother: and it came to pass, when they were in the field, that Cain rose up against Abel his brother, and slew him.*

ⁱⁱ *1 Peter 1:21-25 Who by him do believe in God, that raised him up from the dead, and gave him glory; that your faith and hope might be in God. 22 Seeing ye have purified your souls in obeying the truth through the Spirit unto unfeigned love of the brethren, see that ye love one another with a pure heart fervently: 23 Being born again, not of corruptible seed, but of incorruptible, by the word of God, which liveth and abideth for ever. 24 For all flesh is as grass, and all the glory of man as the flower of grass. The grass withereth, and the flower thereof falleth away: 25 But the word of the Lord endureth for ever. And this is the word which by the gospel is preached unto you.*

ⁱⁱⁱ *John 3:1-23 There was a man of the Pharisees, named Nicodemus, a ruler of the Jews: 2 The same came to Jesus by night, and said unto him, Rabbi, we know that thou art a teacher come from God: for no man can do these miracles that thou doest, except God be with him. 3 Jesus answered and said unto him, Verily, verily, I say unto thee, Except a man be born again, he cannot see the kingdom of God. 4 Nicodemus saith unto him, How can a man be born when he is old? can he enter the second time into his mother's womb, and be born? 5 Jesus answered, Verily, verily, I say unto thee, Except a man be born of water and of the Spirit, he cannot enter into the kingdom of God. 6 That which is born of the flesh is flesh; and that which is born of the Spirit is spirit. 7 Marvel not that I said unto thee,*

Ye must be born again. 8 The wind bloweth where it listeth, and thou hearest the sound thereof, but canst not tell whence it cometh, and whither it goeth: so is every one that is born of the Spirit. 9 Nicodemus answered and said unto him, How can these things be? 10 Jesus answered and said unto him, Art thou a master of Israel, and knowest not these things? 11 Verily, verily, I say unto thee, We speak that we do know, and testify that we have seen; and ye receive not our witness. 12 If I have told you earthly things, and ye believe not, how shall ye believe, if I tell you of heavenly things? 13 And no man hath ascended up to heaven, but he that came down from heaven, even the Son of man which is in heaven. 14 And as Moses lifted up the serpent in the wilderness, even so must the Son of man be lifted up: 15 That whosoever believeth in him should not perish, but have eternal life. 16 For God so loved the world, that he gave his only begotten Son, that whosoever believeth in him should not perish, but have everlasting life. 17 For God sent not his Son into the world to condemn the world; but that the world through him might be saved. 18 He that believeth on him is not condemned: but he that believeth not is condemned already, because he hath not believed in the name of the only begotten Son of God. 19 And this is the condemnation, that light is come into the world, and men loved darkness rather than light, because their deeds were evil. 20 For every one that doeth evil hateth the light, neither cometh to the light, lest his deeds should be reproved. 21 But he that doeth truth cometh to the light, that his deeds may be made manifest, that they are wrought in God. 22 After these things came Jesus and his disciples into the land of Judaea; and there he tarried with them, and baptized. 23 And John also was baptizing in Aenon near to Salim, because there was much water there: and they came, and were baptized.

iv Ephesians 6:10-18 Finally, my brethren, be strong in the Lord, and in the power of his might. 11 Put on the whole armour of God, that ye may be able to stand against the wiles of the devil. 12 For we wrestle not against flesh and blood, but against principalities, against powers, against the rulers of the darkness of this world, against spiritual wickedness in high places. 13 Wherefore take unto you the whole armour of God, that ye may be able to withstand in the evil day, and having done all, to stand. 14 Stand therefore, having your loins girt about with truth, and having on the breastplate of righteousness; 15 And your feet shod with the preparation of the gospel of peace; 16 Above all, taking the shield of faith, wherewith ye shall be able to quench all the fiery darts of the wicked. 17 And take the helmet of salvation, and the sword of the Spirit, which is the word of God: 18 Praying always with all prayer and supplication in the Spirit, and watching thereunto with all perseverance and supplication for all saints;

v 2 *Chronicles 20:1-29 It came to pass after this also, that the children of Moab, and the children of Ammon, and with them other beside the Ammonites, came against Jehoshaphat to battle. 2 Then there came some that told Jehoshaphat, saying, There cometh a great multitude against thee from beyond the sea on this side Syria; and, behold, they be in Hazazontamar, which is Engedi. 3 And Jehoshaphat feared, and set himself to seek the LORD, and proclaimed a fast throughout all Judah. 4 And Judah gathered themselves together, to ask help of the LORD: even out of all the cities of Judah they came to seek the LORD. 5 And Jehoshaphat stood in the congregation of Judah and Jerusalem, in the house of the LORD, before the new court, 6 And said, O LORD God of our fathers, art not thou God in heaven? and rulest not thou over all the kingdoms of the heathen? and in thine hand is there not power and might, so that none is able to withstand thee? 7 Art not thou our God, who didst drive out the inhabitants of this land before thy people Israel, and gavest it to the seed of Abraham thy friend for ever? 8 And they dwelt therein, and have built thee a sanctuary therein for thy name, saying, 9 If, when evil cometh upon us, as the sword, judgment, or pestilence, or famine, we stand before this house, and in thy presence, (for thy name is in this house,) and cry unto thee in our affliction, then thou wilt hear and help. 10 And now, behold, the children of Ammon and Moab and mount Seir, whom thou wouldest not let Israel invade, when they came out of the land of Egypt, but they turned from them, and destroyed them not; 11 Behold, I say, how they reward us, to come to cast us out of thy possession, which thou hast given us to inherit. 12 O our God, wilt thou not judge them? for we have no might against this great company that cometh against us; neither know we what to do: but our eyes are upon thee. 13 And all Judah stood before the LORD, with their little ones, their wives, and their children. 14 Then upon Jahaziel the son of Zechariah, the son of Benaiah, the son of Jeiel, the son of Mattaniah, a Levite of the sons of Asaph, came the Spirit of the LORD in the midst of the congregation; 15 And he said, Hearken ye, all Judah, and ye inhabitants of Jerusalem, and thou king Jehoshaphat, Thus saith the LORD unto you, Be not afraid nor dismayed by reason of this great multitude; for the battle is not yours, but God's. 16 To morrow go ye down against them: behold, they come up by the cliff of Ziz; and ye shall find them at the end of the brook, before the wilderness of Jeruel. 17 Ye shall not need to fight in this battle: set yourselves, stand ye still, and see the salvation of the LORD with you, O Judah and Jerusalem: fear not, nor be dismayed; to morrow go out against them: for the LORD will be with you. 18 And Jehoshaphat bowed his head with his face to the ground: and all Judah and the inhabitants of Jerusalem fell before the LORD, worshipping the LORD. 19 And the Levites, of the children of the Kohathites, and of the children of the Korhites,*

125

stood up to praise the LORD God of Israel with a loud voice on high. 20 And they rose early in the morning, and went forth into the wilderness of Tekoa: and as they went forth, Jehoshaphat stood and said, Hear me, O Judah, and ye inhabitants of Jerusalem; Believe in the LORD your God, so shall ye be established; believe his prophets, so shall ye prosper. 21 And when he had consulted with the people, he appointed singers unto the LORD, and that should praise the beauty of holiness, as they went out before the army, and to say, Praise the LORD; for his mercy endureth for ever. 22 And when they began to sing and to praise, the LORD set ambushments against the children of Ammon, Moab, and mount Seir, which were come against Judah; and they were smitten. 23 For the children of Ammon and Moab stood up against the inhabitants of mount Seir, utterly to slay and destroy them: and when they had made an end of the inhabitants of Seir, every one helped to destroy another. 24 And when Judah came toward the watch tower in the wilderness, they looked unto the multitude, and, behold, they were dead bodies fallen to the earth, and none escaped. 25 And when Jehoshaphat and his people came to take away the spoil of them, they found among them in abundance both riches with the dead bodies, and precious jewels, which they stripped off for themselves, more than they could carry away: and they were three days in gathering of the spoil, it was so much. 26 And on the fourth day they assembled themselves in the valley of Berachah; for there they blessed the LORD: therefore the name of the same place was called, The valley of Berachah, unto this day. 27 Then they returned, every man of Judah and Jerusalem, and Jehoshaphat in the forefront of them, to go again to Jerusalem with joy; for the LORD had made them to rejoice over their enemies. 28 And they came to Jerusalem with psalteries and harps and trumpets unto the house of the LORD. 29 And the fear of God was on all the kingdoms of those countries, when they had heard that the LORD fought against the enemies of Israel.

vi Luke 15:11-31 And he said, A certain man had two sons: 12 And the younger of them said to his father, Father, give me the portion of goods that falleth to me. And he divided unto them his living. 13 And not many days after the younger son gathered all together, and took his journey into a far country, and there wasted his substance with riotous living. 14 And when he had spent all, there arose a mighty famine in that land; and he began to be in want. 15 And he went and joined himself to a citizen of that country; and he sent him into his fields to feed swine. 16 And he would fain have filled his belly with the husks that the swine did eat: and no man gave unto him. 17 And when he came to himself, he said, How many hired servants of my father's have bread enough and to spare, and I perish with hunger! 18 I will arise and go to my father, and will say unto him, Father, I have sinned against heaven, and before thee, 19 And am no more

126

worthy to be called thy son: make me as one of thy hired servants. 20 *And he arose, and came to his father. But when he was yet a great way off, his father saw him, and had compassion, and ran, and fell on his neck, and kissed him.* 21 *And the son said unto him, Father, I have sinned against heaven, and in thy sight, and am no more worthy to be called thy son.* 22 *But the father said to his servants, Bring forth the best robe, and put it on him; and put a ring on his hand, and shoes on his feet:* 23 *And bring hither the fatted calf, and kill it; and let us eat, and be merry:* 24 *For this my son was dead, and is alive again; he was lost, and is found. And they began to be merry.* 25 *Now his elder son was in the field: and as he came and drew nigh to the house, he heard musick and dancing.* 26 *And he called one of the servants, and asked what these things meant.* 27 *And he said unto him, Thy brother is come; and thy father hath killed the fatted calf, because he hath received him safe and sound.* 28 *And he was angry, and would not go in: therefore came his father out, and intreated him.* 29 *And he answering said to his father, Lo, these many years do I serve thee, neither transgressed I at any time thy commandment: and yet thou never gavest me a kid, that I might make merry with my friends:* 30 *But as soon as this thy son was come, which hath devoured thy living with harlots, thou hast killed for him the fatted calf.* 31 *And he said unto him, Son, thou art ever with me, and all that I have is thine.*

Patmos Isle Publishing

www.troyshaw.com

128

Patmos Isle Publishing

www.troyshaw.com

Patmos Isle Publishing

www.troyshaw.com

Patmos (Πάτμος): Somewhere between 81 A.D. and 96 AD, the Apostle John was exiled to the Isle of Patmos (a rugged and bare island in the Aegean Sea); for his commitment to the word of God and testimony of Christ. John wrote the prophecy of Revelation during his island exile. *"Revelation 1:9 - I John, who also am your brother, and companion in tribulation, and in the kingdom and patience of Jesus Christ, was in the isle that is called Patmos, for the word of God, and for the testimony of Jesus Christ."*

Made in the USA
Charleston, SC
29 August 2013